INTRODUCTION

This is a story about one man who like lots of other people struggle with the meaning of life and the ways of the world. From a naïve upbringing during the 1950's to modern day. The road of life, with its twists and turns is sometimes prone to throwing a person off kilter and into depths of disillusionment and depression. But this book is written in order to offer hope, that with a little grit and determination, anyone can stay in the saddle throughout life's experiences and be thoroughly proud of themselves and their own accomplishments.

DISCLAIMER

This a story based upon true events. In order that individuals that are living or dead are not identified. Their names have been changed, and some of the geographical locations have also been altered.

© Copyright 2020 Desmond Brookes
All Rights Reserved.
Protected with www.protectmywork.com,
Reference Number: 9833300420S007

TABLE OF CONTENTS

INTRODUCTION   2

Chapter 1   The Drinkwaters   3

Chapter 2   Donald makes an Entrance   7

Chapter 3   Goodbye to Llangogog   15

Chapter 4   Life after School   20

Chapter 5	Life as a Catering Officer	36
Chapter 6	Medical & Miscellaneous	43
Chapter 7	Political Viewpoint	49
Chapter 8	Life Ashore	53
Chapter 9	Chauffeur Extraordinaire	57
Chapter 10	Donald's Plaice	63
Chapter 11	Back on the Ocean Wave	81
Chapter 12	Donald Weds Penny	85
Chapter 13	Life with Bank Line	89
Chapter 14	Student Inspector	98
Chapter 15	Qualified Inspector	101
Chapter 16	Trip of a Lifetime	106
Chapter 17	Stormy Seas	118
Chapter 18	Walter and the Last Trip	121
Chapter 19	Life Ashore (Again)	124
Chapter 20	Heading toward Retirement	134
Illustrations	77-80, 110-112, 134	
CONCLUSION & DEDICATION		138

CHAPTER 1
THE DRINKWATERS

Beautiful North Wales. Mountains and valleys, rolling countryside and landscapes to suit the palette of any budding artist.

The Drinkwater Family lived in a small town outside of Bangor called Llangogog. A pretty town that the residents took pride in keeping neat and tidy. No real crime in Llangogog, just the usual misdemeanours involving rowdy elements of the younger generation, and litter louts.

The Drinkwater family consisted of a mother, father and three children. Post-war Britain was still feeling the pinch from the fall-out of World War Two, so life was a struggle to make ends meet, with little spare cash about to waste on frills.

Head of the family was Walter, who served in the Royal Navy as a medic during the war. Mother Margo was originally from Glasgow, and had served in a munitions factory in Glasgow throughout the war. Walter and Margo met in August 1945, in Edinburgh during the celebrations of Victory over Japan. Walter's ship had been berthed at Rosyth, and he and his crew mates were ashore and celebrating with all the other revellers.
Margo was with two of her friends from the munitions factory. Walter and Margo were instantly attracted to each other, and it was not long before they were seeing a lot more of each other, and they fell in love. To cut a long story short, they married on Bonfire night in 1947.

Margo's mother was a single mother named Faniella, but everyone called her Fanny. She was a shrew of a woman, very prim and proper, who lived in a small terraced Glasgow corporation house. A woman who held delusions of grandeur. She was a true blue Royalist, and endeavoured to live up to the expectations of the aristocracy, though she struggled with poverty throughout her life. Albeit, her wee house was spotless, as she was a cleaning freak, who spent most of her free time dusting, and then dusting again. Little bowls of boiled sweets and mints used to sit in various places throughout her little abode. (This was in case unexpected guests arrived, and then they could dip into the boiled confectionary and suck happily away). Though poor old Fanny never received many visitors. She considered guests could muck up her spotless home, and she would then have to rush around with a carpet sweeper, wet wipe the furniture, plump up the cushions, ensuring a sterile home.

Fanny approved of Walter, well as much as she could. Fanny had raised Margo as a Barbie doll. All well and good, but poor Margo could not (or was not allowed) to think for herself. Fanny loved Margo, but in a very controlling manner. So Margo grew into womanhood with no real self -belief. Margo was a bright girl as she had passed her eleven plus and had attended a Grammar School. Two things Margo had in abundance was a streak of determination and a stubbornness to match.

Walter understood his mother in law, and realised that if he and Margo were to have an independent life free of Fanny, then they would have to set up home many miles away from Glasgow town. Walter hailed from Somerset. A West - Country lad from humble beginnings. His father, Archibald, was a door to door sales rep who sold Britannica Encyclopaedia's. Archibald was married to Frieda who worked on the shop floor in the pop factory specialising in bottling *Lucozade*. Archibald was a fiery rebel who believed that the distribution of wealth should be shared out equally, he did not believe in the class structure. He grew up at a time, when the rich became richer, and the poor suffered. He was an ardent trade unionist, and had taken part in the 1926 general strike. Archibald was not a man that believed that money maketh the man, he believed that doing your best for your community and struggling to achieve fairness and justice for all, would create a better society. He was a member of the county council and eventually became a Justice of the Peace. There was many a time that he would share any of his meagre wealth with anyone who needed his help. There were occasions where he was left with only threepence in his pocket (much to the disapproval of wife Frieda) who believed that 'charity began at home'.

Walter did well at school, as he also passed his eleven plus and went to a Grammar School. He grew up in a loving family. His Dad was a good role model, and his mother doted on him. Walter did not know for sure what he wanted to do for a living, but felt that he would like to work on the health of people's feet, and his goal was to become a chiropodist. He studied with determination and trained hard and became a fully qualified chiropodist.

When Walter married Margo in 1947, they lived for a while in a bedsit near his parents' home in the village of Green Bottom, Somerset. Walter spotted an advert for the position of chiropodist in a private clinic in the town of Llangogog in North Wales. Walter was not flush with funds, and this position offered a cottage as residence within the grounds of the clinic.

Walter sent off his CV with a covering letter and within the week, he was offered an interview. He landed the job. He was as pleased as Punch that at last he could ensure that both he and Margo would be settled, and they could start a new adventure together.

So, in March 1948, Walter and Margo set off for Llangogog. Taking the train from Taunton to Bangor via Liverpool. They took a bus from Bangor to Langogog, and were thrilled to see that their new home was not just a cottage, but a large four bed detached property in an acre of garden. The cottage was beautiful. It had a large comfortable lounge, a dining room, another ground floor room that would eventually become a playroom for the kids. A massive kitchen with a range, and a walk in pantry that would be the size of a kitchen in the homes of today. A large bathroom upstairs, and four massive bedrooms. This was really a step up from the dingy bed-sit in Green Bottom.

Walter and Margo settled into domestic bliss in Llangogog. Margo took a job at the corner shop, where she enjoyed meeting the populace of Llangogog, though she had difficulty with understanding the Welsh accent, and the fact that some of her customers could not speak English at all, and only could converse in Welsh. This resulted in a lot of gesticulation from both parties and pidgin English from Margo.

Walter was welcomed at the clinic and he met many stars and celebrities, the famous and the wealthy. Anyone that could afford private treatment, were able to push the boat out when it came to paying the earth to preserve health. He enjoyed working on the many gnarled and bunioned tootsies of the rich.

In October 1948, Walter and Margo were expecting their first baby Drinkwater. The pregnancy was non eventful, and Margo continued working at the corner shop until late June 1949. With great joy, they were blessed with a son on 14 July 1949. Although Walter was not a politik like his father Archibald, he possessed a little of the red, inherited from his father. A baby boy was born on Bastille Day, Walter wanted to call him Robespierre, the rebel of all rebels who liked lopping people's heads off at the Guillotine. Well Margo was not having any of this, she did not want any son of hers named after a French maniac who enjoyed terrorizing the public, just for the fun of it. So Margo said to Walter "We will call our little cherub, Ronald." Walter caved in and agreed, as Margo preferred the banality of a Ronald to a Robespierre in the family.

Walter doted on little Ronald. The boy was born with curly blond hair, rosy cheeks, blue eyes and the countenance of a cherub. Ronald soon leaned, like most babies, that he was the big cheese in the Drinkwater family, and he used his wiles to get anything he wanted. Ronald realised how easy it was to manipulate people.

Whilst Walter and Margo had settled down quite nicely into domestic bliss in Langogog. Good old mother in law, Fanny from Glasgow had been feeling quite out of the picture since her new son-in-law had whisked her Barbie Doll daughter away from the Gorbels. Fanny had spent 28 years controlling Margo, and it was no easy job breaking away from this habit.

Especially when you have no other real interests in life, other than filling up the sweet bowls with Everton Mints and Humbugs. And there is only so much dusting a girl can do.

So with that in mind, Fanny packed her cardboard suitcase and decided to cast off her Scottish roots and become a fully-fledged Welshie. How hard can it be? Though she thought "I can't do this on my own". Cutting a long story short. The lovely Fanny managed to hook herself a younger man, a Geordie from Newcastle called Humphrey. Humphrey was the salt of the earth. A veteran of the eighth army under the command of Field Marshal Bernard Montgomery. Humphrey fought in the North African campaigns. After the war, he found work in Glasgow and set up a small garage business where he serviced cars. He was a brilliant engineer, and even built a three wheel car from scratch, before they were seen on the roads as Reliant Robins. Humphrey was taken in by Fanny's charms. She knew how to manipulate, and she could be a mistress manipulator to anyone when she set her heart on the task in hand.

She had never divorced her husband (mother of Margo).Her hubby was an alcoholic and preferred the Glasgow Gin joints to snuggling up with Fanny in the evening. Fanny had put up with him for five years of marriage, and she considered hubby to be a complete waste of space, she also thought that his personal hygiene left a lot to be desired! This was no life for a woman born for pomp and grandeur. So one night, when hubby returned home bladdered, singing "My heart belongs to Glasgow, dear old Glasgow town". Fanny had packed a bag for him, she had garnered £75.00 saved from her meagre earnings as a shop girl. She gave hubby the cash on the condition that he leaves her for good and would never to darken her doorway again, kicking him out of the marital home. He was never to be seen again. He is likely to have drunk himself to death, but who knows….

So Fanny could not marry Humphrey as she was still legally married. She and Humphrey decided to shack up together and pretend to be married. She had her name changed by deed poll to Humphrey's surname of Ballstock, and they became the very respectable Mr & Mrs Ballstock.

Mr & Mrs Ballstock arrived in Llangogog and rented a small house in the town. Humphrey managed to buy a disused building, and converted it into a garage, setting up business servicing cars for the local populace. Needless to say, son-in law Walter was none too fussed to have mother in law living in close proximity, as it was soon apparent that she would be doing a lot of interfering, and picking up where she had left off and controlling Margo, undermining her sense of wellbeing for her own gratification.

CHAPTER 2
Donald makes an Entrance

Walter and Margo celebrated the birth of their second son. Donald made his appearance on 20 August 1950. Margo always had a soft spot for the British Speed Record Breaker Donald Campbell, so without further ado, and very little consultation with Walter, the boy was called Donald. Walter was not too concerned about the name or indeed much else about his second son. First son Ronald was still the apple of his eye. When Margo brought Donald home from hospital, she introduced the new arrival to Ronald. Ronald took one look at Donald, and was not impressed, thinking "Hey, this looks like competition, and there isn't enough room for this interloper". So, with that in mind Ronald was not in the frame of mind to compromise his top dog position within the household. It was obvious that Walter was still well and truly wrapped up with Ronald.

The Drinkwater family settled in with the busy schedule involved with raising two children and only 13 months between the ages of both boys. Margo was run ragged, she was not a natural domestic. Having been brought up by a mother who was self-absorbed with pomp and snobbery, and believed that if everything looked okay on the surface, then any muck that can be seen, can be swept under the carpet.

Fanny visited Margo as often as she could, and usually turned up at the Drinkwater family home around four of five times in a week, offering advice on child-rearing, without actually getting herself too involved in the process. Margo was pleased to see her mother, though she was programmed to accept her mother's presence, and never considered that her Fanny was anything but a support and help. Fanny was happy that her beloved daughter had produced two grandchildren, though Fanny would have preferred that they were girls, rather than boys. She remembered the joy raising Margo, dressing Margo, brushing and plaiting her hair. It was just like having a dolly. Lots and lots of endless fun. It wouldn't be as much fun with wretched little boys. Fanny encouraged Margo to keep trying and to produce a little girl.

Not sure why Walter and Margo never considered giving themselves some breathing space, as life wasn't busy enough bringing up two boys with only thirteen months difference in their ages. It could have been that, as they had found their rhythm in the love-making department, they had no clue on how to stop, and to plan a family sensibly. So eighteen months had passed since the birth of Donald, and Margo gave birth on 8 April 1952 to a bouncing baby girl. With lots of whooping, especially from Fanny at this wonderful gift from God, the Drinkwater family were now complete. The new addition was called by the homely name of 'Elsie'. She was a beautiful child with dark hair in ringlets, bright blue eyes and a fresh complexion. Elsie would have been a great advert for Pears Soap.

All looked really normal in the Drinkwater household. Mum, Dad and three lovely children. However, there were undercurrents on how to cope with bringing up children to adulthood. The journey looked daunting indeed, and it was becoming more of a chore than a natural choice, as time moved on. So how can 'damage limitation' be managed successfully, so that both parents can survive the ordeal without too much suffering?

As Margo had not learned the basics involved with the kitchen, such as cooking and baking food, she was adrift to the simple mechanics of understanding a recipe. This was of course mostly due to Fanny not imparting domestic knowledge to her daughter. After all, why would a pretty, beautiful Barbie Doll need to know such things? The main aim was just to be pretty and obedient.

Margo tried her hand at baking a cake using the lovely range in her super kitchen. She carefully read the instructions, mixing up the butter and sugar, then adding the eggs, and then finally adding the sifted flour, and a few drops of milk. Popping the mixture into the oven, ensuring that the heat was 180 degrees as per the recipe, she left the cake to bake for 30 minutes. The minutes ticked by, and there was a nervous energy in the kitchen, as both Walter and Margo were cock a hoop that they were in the process of baking their very first cake together. Within 22 minutes, smoke started emitting from the oven. Walter was becoming agitated, whilst Margo remained calm. The smoke was becoming blacker and thicker by the minute. After 28 minutes, both Walter and Margo were having difficulty with their breathing, they could hardly see each other. Walter screamed "Get the cake out Margo!" "No, no,no" yelled Margo in return. "It says 30 minutes on the recipe, not 28 minutes!" Margo opens the door on exactly 30 minutes baking time, and with much coughing and spluttering, Margo produces a smoking black mass of charcoal, that was supposed to have been a vanilla sponge. "Oh well" said Walter, "When it's brown it's done, but when it's black, it's buggered."

That was Margo's first and last attempt at baking. It was all too difficult. After all, isn't it better not to think, than struggle with the complexities of cooking? This catering malarkey was all too much trouble.

Walter was more practical in the kitchen, and could make a mean Macaroon. He also enjoyed churning out mince pies every Christmas.

The 1950's were lean times for many families throughout the Kingdom. The country was still coming to terms with poverty and a collapsed economy brought on by the tragedy of the Second World War. The Drinkwater family struggled along with everyone else. Whereas when Walter was growing up in a working class environment during the 1920's, his parents made sure that they always provided nutritious food and nourishment in the home. Stews, roast joints of meat (when affordable), fish and vegetables and potatoes were the order of the day. Margo was brought up on similar fare, but Margo provided the simplest of food for her own children. Biscuits, cakes, soups and the like.

When Donald was five, he was enrolled at the Llangogog Primary School. Ronald had already been at school for a full year. Donald had not given the idea of school attendance much thought, so it came as a bit of a surprise when Walter took both boys to school. Walter led Donald into a classroom, and talked to the teacher, Miss Smith, a grey haired mature lady. Walter then left the classroom telling Donald to stay put. The class consisted of around 15 boys and girls, and the children were all sat down in pairs behind desks. Miss Smith showed Donald where he was to sit, which was alongside another little boy. Donald looked down at the little boy sitting looking up at him, and Donald, shook his head, and said to Miss Smith "No." Miss Smith coaxed Donald to sit as requested, but Donald was adamant. He was not definitely not going to sit down. After all, in his mind, he did not expect to be staying at school very long anyway. Miss Smith then said to Donald that he could stand by the desk for as long as he liked. Donald agreed, and stood there all day.
This was definitely a stubborn streak that Donald had inherited from his mother. The stubbornness could be seen as determined and resolute by some, or by others as tedious and time-wasting. Donald just saw it as being Donald.

One day at school, Donald was attending class, and a nice lady teacher called Mrs Thomas was taking the class. Donald was sat behind a desk as the back of the classroom, and he pulled out a Dinky Toy from his pocket. It was a beige pick-up truck, just like Grandpop Humphrey used for going to work. Donald liked Grandpop Humphrey as he was always very kind to him, and in those days Donald needed all the help and support that he could get. Donald was running the little Dinky toy up and down the desk quite happily amusing himself. Mrs Thomas then noticed that he was not paying full attention to the lesson in hand, and asked Donald to put the toy away and to pay attention. He put the little van away in his pocket. However, he did not think that Mrs Thomas' lesson was very interesting, in fact it was more than a little boring, so he pulled the van out again and ran it up and down his desk. Mrs Thomas, had had enough by this time, so she told Donald to leave the classroom, to cross the yard and go and see the Headmistress Miss Smith and tell her that Mrs Thomas had sent him to her for a lesson in discipline.

Donald got up from his desk, and walked out of the classroom, and then he crossed the yard, went around the corner, where he waited, hidden from view for around five minutes. He then returned to the classroom. Mrs Thomas asked Donald if he had seen Miss Smith. Donald replied "Yes." Mrs Thomas asked him what Miss Smith had said to him. Donald replied "Oh she said that everything was alright." Mrs Thomas then asked him to sit down for the rest of the lesson.

However, during break-time, Mrs Thomas went to see Miss Smith, and it soon became obvious that Donald had been telling fibs, and indeed had not been to see Miss Smith at all. He was called into Miss Smith's classroom, and he was ordered to stand facing the corner for 30 minutes .Donald learned that if you were going to tell a fib, then you had to be more careful in the future not to get found out!

Brother Ronald was doing fine at school, a year ahead of Donald. When Ronald was around 8 years old, Miss Smith, the head teacher was updating her school files, and wanted to know the profession of parents. She asked Ronald what his father did for a living. Well Ronald had not given his father's occupation any real thought, so he had no idea at all. Miss Smith thought well if Ronald didn't know, then she would have to ask Donald, though, as she already had a few run ins with Donald, she was not too hopeful that he would know which day of the week it was, never mind his father's profession. Well it was worth a try. She asked Donald the question, and he immediately piped up "He's a Chiropodist Miss!" Although people assumed that Donald may not be quite the full shilling, he did prove to have a very good memory, and although he was a quiet boy, he did listen to what was going on around him.

Walter treated wealthy patients at the private clinic where he worked, and sometimes his patients used to come to the house. They were charmed by the Drinkwater family, as Walter put on his best face of respectability, and the family looked to be an endearing and close knit unit. One old gent and his wife Mr & Mrs McTaggerty used to visit in their Rolls Royce and would stay for tea and biscuits with the Drinkwater's. The McTaggerty's never had any children, so they took a keen interest in Ronald, Donald and Elsie. This lovely couple would bring the boys toy rifles, and for Elsie a dolly, and sometimes sweets and lollipops. Another old man, who was very wealthy used to visit, called Frank Yeomans. A really nice old gent. One day he gave each of the Drinkwater children an envelope, and inside each envelope was a note with an inscription and instructions. If the inscription could be read three times without stumbling over the words, then each child would win ten shillings. Donald's inscription was 'Around the rugged rock, the ragged rascal ran' Donald was pleased to recite this phrase three times, without stumbling over the words, and he was rewarded gleefully with a ten shilling note.

On another day when the three children had been given half a crown each by a wealthy patient. They were all playing outside in the garden, and Donald clumsily dropped his half-crown into the grass on the lawn. Ronald came over to see that the fuss was about, and offered to help Donald look for the coin. Little did Donald know that Ronald had already spotted the coin in the long grass, and had immediately put his foot on it, still pretending to look for the missing money! After a while, the search was given up and Donald was depressed that he had carelessly lost his money, and thought that he must be more careful in the future. However, Ronald was delighted, he had found a way of making easy money and a 100% profit in the process.

For the Drinkwater children, food was simple and repetitive. During school term, Breakfast consisted of a small bowl of cornflakes and a cup of tea. Half a pint of milk was provide free at the primary school during the mid-morning playtime. Then there was school lunch, costing a shilling a day. Nice and nutritious hot food consisting of a main course and a hot dessert such as spotted dick and custard.

Teatime at home every day from five years old to sixteen years old was always the same. Consisting of white sliced bread, spread with a mix of butter and margarine, three tea-time assorted biscuits and a slice of Battenburg cake with a cup of tea. Ronald and Elsie where allowed to put jam on their bread, whilst Donald was permitted Marmalade. Donald, like Paddington Bear enjoyed Marmalade sandwiches very much. Just as well, as he wasn't allowed Jam.

School holidays were a challenge as there were no school dinners. So, especially during the six week summer holidays, hunger was never too far away. Margo provided a hard- boiled egg for each child at lunch times.

Weekends were another challenge in staving off any hunger pangs. As Margo had given up trying to cook since the debacle of the cake baking exercise. Cooked food was definitely off the menu, and it was either cold food, boiled egg, or as a special treat on a Sunday, there was tinned vegetable soup, which consisted of a ratio of one cup of soup diluted by one cup of water. Donald did ask his mother once if she could possibly consider changing the routine from serving vegetable soup to chicken soup. He had noticed the option when he had accompanied Margo on a previous shopping trip. Margo rejected this request out of hand. Vegetable soup is what she was used to boiling up, and the very thought of experimenting with another soup was totally out of the question. Well it was worth a try!

Hunger, and the thought of food played on the minds of the children a lot of the time. Donald was sitting alone in the lounge one day, and noticed that there was one rosy red apple sitting all on its own, in a polished wooden fruit bowl on the broad window sill. Donald's eyes kept darting back to that lonely apple, and as the minutes ticked by, there was more and more of an urge to at least nibble that lovely piece of fresh fruit. He approached the apple, picked it up and looking lovingly at it, he put it to his mouth, and with the very smallest of bites, nibbled a minute piece of skin from the apple. Chewing slowly on this slither of rind and tasting the slightest trace of sweetness. Putting the apple back in the bowl, with the nibbled evidence hidden as much as possible.

Next day, at the same time in the afternoon, Donald was back in the lounge, and the apple was still sitting in the fruit bowl. "Just another little nibble won't hurt, will it?" thought Donald. So he picked up the apple and nibbled another small minute piece, savouring again the sweet nutrition. This routine went on for another three consecutive days, until it was virtually impossible to hide the nibbled aspects of the apple. It was only a matter of time and the game would be up, and indeed, it was when Walter came across the mutilated apple.

Walter gathered all three children into the lounge and announced, that whoever nibbled the apple must own up to the crime. Ronald, Donald and Elsie were rooted to the sofa. Ronald and Elsie where blameless and knew nothing of this misdemeanour. Walter was by now getting very agitated, as he wanted to know who had carried out this dastardly deed. Well, Donald had no inclination to enlighten him, as he knew that the consequence would be a severe beating. In the end, Walter gave up as no one was ever going to own up. In order to teach a lesson to all three, the children were banned from the normal schedule of 30 minutes TV viewing of the Whirlybirds, a series on everyday life, about the crew of a helicopter.

Phew, Donald breathed a sigh of relief. He had survived a bashing.

Walter had a special name he gave to all three children. Ronald was called Faith, Donald was called Hope, and Elsie was named Charity. In order to curry favour with his father, Donald innocently asked Walter why his pet name was Hope. Walter replied "Well Donald, that's easy, Hope is short for hopeless!"

Donald was not too happy with this variation on the word hope, and wondered why Walter couldn't find a reason to be kinder.

By the time Donald was six, and Ronald was seven. Ronald continued to resented Donald, and found it quite amusing to make life as uncomfortable as he could for him. Ronald knew that he alone held the heart of his father, and that in real terms he maintained the title of top dog. But in order to ensure that top dog status would be maintained, he had to devise new schemes in order to keep Donald in the Doghouse.

Ronald and Donald shared a double bed in one room. Ronald thought of a novel idea on making the middle of the night more entertaining. Ronald decided to pull off all the bedclothes from the bed, so pillows, sheets and blankets were thrown to the floor. This woke up Donald, who could not imagine what was taking place. Donald then could hear Ronald yelling for their father. Walter burst into the room where Ronald told him that Donald was to blame for being manic and throwing the bedclothes to the floor. Well Donald could have defended himself, and said that he was not the culprit, but he knew even at the age of six, that he was not likely to be believed, as in Walter's eyes, Ronald could do no wrong.

So Donald kept quiet. Walter looked at Donald, thinking that maybe he should have been named Damien instead of Donald. Walter made up the boys' bed in good order, letting Ronald get back into the bed, and kissing him affectionately on the cheek. Walter turned to Donald, and said "Put your Dressing Gown on Donald, and come with me!" Donald followed his father out of the room, and Walter ordered him to sit on the landing. "That is where you will stay Donald, for the rest of the night!" Walter then returned to his own room, leaving Donald to contemplate the complexities of growing up in a dysfunctional family.

Ronald kept up the same episode on a nightly basis, even when Donald pleaded with him to give it a rest. Ronald would promise that he would not pull the bed clothes off again, but within an hour it was de ja vous, and Donald would spend another cold night on the landing.

During this period Ronald and Donald where both watching TV on a Saturday afternoon in the lounge. Saturday was the day that Margo and Elsie went to see Nanna Fanny at her house where they spent the afternoon for an all girlie time with afternoon tea. The boys' were not allowed to go to Nanna Fanny's house. Fanny only liked the company of girls in her family.

So Saturday was a day when Walter looked after Ronald and Donald. Whilst watching TV, and Walter was in the kitchen. Ronald said to Donald, whilst reaching out for a burning stick from the open fire. "Do you think this will hurt Donald?" Before he could answer, Ronald had stuck the point of the flaming stick into the bare left foot of Donald. Donald let out a howl of pain, and looked down to see that the skin on his foot had shrivelled and there was a hole in the top of his foot. Walter, upon hearing the commotion, ran into the lounge. Looking from side to side for an explanation,

Ronald exclaimed "Donald did it to himself!" Walter looked at Donald, and the child noticed that any disclaimer to this allegation was futile, so he accepted the inevitable. Walter cleaned and bandaged Donald's foot, but in Walter's mind he thought that Donald was at best a benign mental case, and hoped that would not grow up to become a complete and raving lunatic.

To make matters worse, as Donald realised that as any sane person would suspect that he was not quite the full shilling, he decided to try and patch things up with his father.

Donald decided to wrench lots of flowers from the flowerbeds in the garden. He picked up as many as he could hold, and took them to his father, saying "These are for you!" Walter by now was completely exasperated, and went berserk shouting at Donald that he was a bloody idiot and a complete head case. Donald thought that it was time to get back to the drawing board.

Ronald and Donald shared bath-time together. Walter would do the honours of washing the boys' hair in the bath. Walter enjoyed pouring water from a plastic jug over Donald's head. The problem was that for Donald it felt more like water boarding rather than a pleasant bath-time experience. That desperate feeling of drowning with a continuous cascade of water falling over the head and face. Donald's panic encouraged Walter to continue with the water boarding, which resulted in a long lasting condition of claustrophobia.

On another Saturday when Margo and Elsie where on their usual visit to Nanna Fanny's house. The boys' played at home. Running through the kitchen, Ronald notices a chocolate sponge cake on the kitchen table. He picks up a table knife, lopping off a chunk of cake, gobbling it up. Thirty minutes later Walter comes into the kitchen and notices that the cake has been hacked. He rounds up the two boys, wanting to determine which one of the boys is the culprit. Ronald immediately pipes up "It was Donald!" Walter turns to Donald and without verifying that Donald was indeed the culprit, he then picked the boy up by the scruff of his neck and the seat of his pants and marched to the garden fence, where on the other side, was a field of bullocks. Walter hauled Donald over the fence, dangling him in mid- air. Walter shouting, "I will feed you to the bullocks! I will feed you to the bullocks!" After what seemed like an eternity, Walter put Donald back down into the garden, while he himself tried to calm his own jangled nerves.

Walter loved Ronald. It was no wonder, as Ronald had the charm, looks and natural talent to please both strangers and relations alike. He was a boy that everyone could warm to. Donald used to wonder why he could not achieve the same popularity. Well Donald was a totally different type of boy, although a good looking little chap, people did not warm to him as they did his brother. Donald was not jealous of his brother's popularity, in fact he was more in awe of Ronald than anything else. It would just have been nice if he himself could have some of that special gold dust.

Bed time was every-night at 7pm, without fail. Each night as everyone sat as a family in the kitchen. At a quarter to seven the radio broadcasted the daily soap 'The Archers', and at 7pm when the signature tune struck up was their cue to go to bed.

Walter used to come up to say goodnight. He always found time to play with Ronald, tickling him and then tucking him into bed, but Donald could never fathom why Walter never seemed bothered at all with him.

Ronald was a true capitalist, he could make money with very little effort, though he also had a flair for cutting corners. When Donald gave him sixpence to go to the corner shop and buy sweets, Ronald was gone for some-time, but returned home. Donald asked Ronald if he had bought the sweets, Ronald said that he had indeed bought the sweets. Well that was the good news. The bad news was that Ronald could not find the sweets that Donald had wanted. Donald accepted that it seemed to be better than nothing. But in fact, it was nothing, because Ronald then informed Donald, he had already eaten the sweets!

Both Ronald and Donald were members of the Langogog Cub Scout Group. The time came for 'Bob a Job' week. This is when cubs go to peoples' houses and ask if they perform a task, and then be paid a shilling. The job could be washing a car, mowing a lawn, shopping, or any other type of domestic chore. Akela, the cub boss told the Cub Pack, that the cub who made the most money, would win the star prize. A Brownie 127 Camera! The star prize appealed to both Ronald and Donald. They set off on their challenge. Donald was determined to win over his brother and knuckled down to work really hard and win that camera.

Donald bumped into Ronald on the housing estates, and Donald found Ronald licking on a 99 Ice cream cone. Most of Ronald's customers would look upon his cherubic countenance when he knocked at their door, and immediately, their hearts would melt. They told him that he did not have to do a job at all, and would give him two shillings just for turning up!

Whereas Donald on the other hand would knock on a door, and on sight, the home owner would then instruct him to mow their lawn, or polish all the shoes of the household, and then he would receive the minimal shilling for his labours.

Donald learned a lesson in that hard work does not always pay off. Ronald eventually won the challenge and was top cub, who was presented with the Brownie 127 camera. Donald was second in the pack, coming up threepence short of the prize.

Although money was tight in the Drinkwater family and food rationing was now a thing of the past, the Drinkwater's were still in rationing mode. One day, there was a knock on the door, and two burly men had arrived delivering an upright piano. Walter had purchased the piano for £5.00 though no one in the family could play the instrument. In hindsight, the £5.00 paid for a piano should have been spent on basics such as food.

As Ronald and Elsie had no interest whatsoever in learning how to play the piano. Donald on the other hand thought it would be nice to be able learn to play a musical instrument. So Walter sourced a music teacher called Mrs Pughes. A jolly rotund middle aged lady who had a little studio in Llangogog. Donald went for music lessons once a week to the studio. His first lesson was 'I am C middle C' not much of a tune to it, but he improved each week, though he had to practice alone in the lounge whilst the family stayed in the kitchen. After each lesson when it was time for Donald to leave. Mrs Pughes, used to say "Donald, what have you forgotten?" It was then that Donald remembered that he had to kiss Mrs Pughes on the cheek to say goodbye.

CHAPTER 3
GOODBYE TO LLANGOGOG

In 1950, the Private Clinic where Walter was the Chief Chiropodist went bankrupt. This meant that Walter lost his job, and not only his job, but the home that came with the job. It was not going to be easy. However, Walter applied through the NHS and accepted into Ysbyty Gwynedd which is a hospital in Bangor. Walter also put s deposit down on a new home in Bangor, a small 3 bed semi-detached property with a small front garden and back garden. A bit of come down with regard to space. The property was purchased for the sum of £2,750.00.

The Drinkwaters moved to Bangor. The two boys attended Bangor High School as they had unfortunately failed their eleven plus exams and therefore could not attend Grammar School like their mother and father. Elsie went to the local primary school.

Ronald excelled in sports. He was an avid fan of Everton Football Club, and a framed picture of Alan Ball adorned our bedroom wall in the new house. Ronald could play 'upsie' for hours on end, which involved kicking a ball from one foot to the other without letting it drop to the ground. He was very adept at this game.
 Donald was not interested in sport, and in fact was hopeless at anything sport oriented. He enjoyed music and art, and would draw and sketch for hours, totally absorbed. Donald also enjoyed politics and history. He excelled at school in history and was always top of his class. He could remember dates very easily. Donald was also top of the class in art, and the art teacher used to allow him free rein to enjoy the subject to the full.

Life was still a struggle for the Drinkwater children. Summer holiday pangs of hunger where difficult times. Once Donald and Elsie had wandered to the local general store, and they looked in through the window and saw a lovely chocolate cake. It really looked tasty, both Donald and Elsie pressed their little noses against the window and savoured the view of that lovely cake. Mrs Gee, the owner, noticed their avid stare through the window, and could see the target of their desire. She saw that both children looked very skinny indeed, and in an act of kindness, she brought out two pieces of the chocolate cake on paper plates for the children to eat. Donald and Elsie had never known such kindness and thanked her, running off and gobbling the cake down in double time.

At the age of eleven and in order to make some pocket money, Donald took a morning newspaper round at the local newsagents. The store was managed by a Mr Cossak and a Mr Pubert. Mr Cossak was an expansive gregarious man, aged around 40 with a wife and two daughters. Mr Cossack believed himself to be an entrepreneur extraordinaire. He thought of himself as a legend, but only in his own mind. After all he was part owner of a newsagents!
The newspaper round was a six day week job, and paid 15 shillings a week. Ronald eventually joined the newspaper boy team and had a round of his own at the same rate of pay. Mr Cossack liked Ronald and played him up to be the best paperboy out of all the boys. Mr Cossack filled the boys' heads with what he could do for them to make their jobs even better. He suggested heated jackets for the winter months. That sounded good to everyone. Unfortunately it was just 'hot air' and no hot jackets materialised. Just another fantasy story from Mr Cossak.
Donald took on another paper round for the evening to deliver the Bangor Times and Manchester Evening News. The job was a six day week at a shilling a day, making Donald a full £1.00 wage per week. The only drawback was that ten shillings was paid to Margo his mother for lodgings, and toward school dinners, which was five shillings a week.

Donald went shopping for Margo one week, and borrowed a bicycle from the butcher with a basket on the handlebars. All went well with the shopping, however on his return home which was down a steep hill, Donald followed a car, which braked and came to a sudden stop. Donald's bike went straight into the back of the car, he somersaulted over the handlebars and landed on the car roof. The shopping was scattered all over the road, and passing cars crunched the cornflakes into smithereens. Although Donald came out of the accident without any serious injury, just some bruising to the nether regions. The front wheel of the bike was well and truly buckled.

Margo was not pleased that the ten shillings worth of shopping had been destroyed in the accident. Though she found a way to recoup the loss. She instructed Donald that he was to hand over his full wage of £1.00 from his newspaper jobs to cover the loss. For the next week he had no money at all to put in his own pocket.

Donald continued with his two paper rounds, whilst Ronald held on to his morning paper round. On the evening paper round Donald used to see his brother hanging around the local fish and chip shop with his mates, and used to wonder why Ronald appeared to be wasting his time with such a boring occupation. It did not seem to be a leisure aspect that was entirely fulfilling.

Donald took a job with the local general store boss, by cleaning Mr Johansson's car on a weekly basis. This job used to raise seven shillings and sixpence, and this was good pay in comparison to the newspaper rounds.

At about the age of thirteen, Donald took an extra job at the local fish and chip shop a a spud peeler. The shop was owned by an Italian couple, called Mr & Mrs Labella. They also owned a second Fish and chip Shop at the top of the town, and Donald eventually started a job there as well. So his day started at 6am with a bowl of cornflakes, then the morning paper round, coming home and changing into his school uniform and going to school for 9am. He would return home just before 4pm, and starting an hour's work at the fish and chip, finishing at 5pm, and then starting the evening paper round and finishing that at 6pm. He would then cycle to the top of town to Mr Labella's other Fish and Chip Shop for another hour of potato bashing. Coming home just after 7pm for homework and bed.

One Saturday whilst Donald was working in the morning peeling spuds at Mrs Labella's Fish and Chip Shop, she sent him out to buy a bag of sugar, and she gave him a reward of two shillings. Mrs Labella liked Donald. On another Saturday after Donald's shift, Mrs Labella was in the middle of wrapping Fish and Chips as a treat for Donald. But Mr Labella turned up unexpectedly, and seeing what his wife was in the middle of doing, he went into a fit of rage, shouting at her in his heavily accented English "Why you give the boy Fish and Chips? You give the boy black pudding!" Mrs Labella did not have the heart to change the fish, so gave the Fish and Chips to Donald. He was pleased with the Fish and Chips, but in reality had no problem with eating black pudding. In those days, Donald was grateful for anything.

Returning to Fanny and Humphrey. Humphrey was a talented man, who was practical and could turn his hand to anything. Although he was a silent figure behind the determined Fanny. Humphrey negotiated a deal by purchasing a derelict house unbeknown to Fanny. He set about in his spare time turning it into a dream home. The house was situated in the countryside outside of Bangor. A beautiful detached remote bungalow with lots of garden space and stunning views.
Fanny was thrilled. Now she had become someone, a lady! Not just a lady but a respectable lady with her own country estate.

Humphrey and Fanny visited Walter and Margo at their house in Bangor, and it was on one of these occasions when Walter and Margo were discussing Donald, and their worry in that he was a wayward boy who was always in mischief, whereas Ronald was the most perfect son, blond, blue-eyed and beautiful. When Humphrey and Fanny were returning home from the Drinkwater's. Humphrey said to Fanny "It's not Donald who's the bad boy, it's all down to Ronald!" Humphrey was very astute and nobody's fool. Of course nobody would believe Grandpop Humphrey.

It was evident that Grandpop Humphrey liked Donald, so both Ronald and Elsie were pleased to be favoured by Nanna Fanny whilst Donald could be lumped with Grandpop Humphrey. Both Ronald and Elsie considered Grandpop Humphrey to be a bit of a bore.

During this period Walter had settled into his job at the hospital. He was no longer just beautifying the feet of the rich and the well to do, he was dealing with the feet of the masses. Margo's health in the meantime was spinning into a downward spiral. She had given up work completely and spent most of her free time sitting in the dining room listening to the Jimmy Young Show on Radio 2, and reading Mills & Boon Romantic novels. This constant inactivity made it difficult for her to walk, and her health deteriorated, she piled on the pounds, and developed an under active thyroid gland condition.

In preparation for the children returning from school. Margo would butter the bread, set out three rows of Battenburg cake, three biscuits onto a plate. Putting a jar of marmalade and a jar of jam on the table. It was all a dreadful chore, and when Margo was in a black mood, she would scream at the children, saying she wondered why she ever had children in the first place, as they were too much bother!

In the Drinkwater family, the parents and children did not eat at the same time. Walter & Margo would eat an hour of two after the children. The menu for parents consisted of food that had been heated, though the nutritious value was below par. Before Walter returned home from work, Margo would go into the kitchen and open a pack of Birds Eye meat rissoles. These were a frozen meat based product covered in breadcrumbs. Margo would put some lard into a frying pan and heat the lard, then plonk two rissoles into the pan to fry. She never seemed to master the art of shallow frying, and the end result, were rissoles that were dark brown in colour, turning blacker, as Margo would switch off the gas ring, and the rissoles would continue to burn and dry out while she returned to reading her Mills & Boone novel.

Walter would come home and sit at the table with Margo. Walter enjoyed using his cloth napkin that lay ready for him, encased in a silver napkin ring. He would flap the napkin and put it onto his lap with a flourish. He would then chisel into his rissoles, served with slices of bread and butter. He would smile at Margo from across the table and say "Very nice dear."

Walter's mother and father would travel from Somerset to North Wales to visit the Drinkwater's for short holiday breaks. Grandad Archibald and Nanna Frieda were the perfect guests complying fully with the abnormality of life in the Welsh Drinkwater family. Waiting expectantly at the Dining Room table for a sumptuous meal at the hands of Margo. Regrettably their high expectations would ultimately lead to disappointment at the very least. The look on Archibald's face was truly very amusing through the eyes of young

Donald. When Margo put a plate of rissoles in front of him, and then return to the kitchen. Archibald looked at the rissoles with incredulity. They sat on his plate, not golden brown and flat, but charcoal black and curled at the edges. Archibald picked up his table fork, and putting the fork under one rissole, he flicked it, and with a somersault flip, it landed with not a meaty thump, but a distinct clatter on the plate. Archibald murmured "what is this supposed to be?" Needless to say he went without dinner that night. His dentures would not have been up to the task.

Donald was friends with a boy in the same class at school called Robin. Both boys were walking home from school one day, and Robin tells Donald that his mother is cooking beef stew and dumplings for his tea. Donald thought this was extraordinary, as he supposed that all children had the same rations of bread, butter and biscuits. And Robin lived in a council house!
One time when Donald was in the science class at school. There was a boy in the class called David Floyd. David was a wow with the girls as they all fancied him. He was a pin up with good looks and always smartly dressed. Where Donald's shirt collar was frayed, and looked like he had been dragged through a hedge backwards. David on the other hand, wore a crisp white shirt and smart Blazer with pressed black trousers and shiny black shoes. David started teasing Donald by flicking compressed paper from a plastic ruler at him. The teacher was out of the room, and David continued the flicking game though he could see that Donald was getting really pissed off. As there appeared no end to the tease, Donald rounded on David and started pummelled him hard in the face with his fists. David tried choking Donald with his own tie. The teacher could be heard returning to the classroom, and the scuffle came to an abrupt end. The teacher looked at Donald with the scrunched up tie and then at David with the two black eyes, and asked "Everything Okay here?" To which they both replied that all was well.
Needless to say that after the science class and when the girls heard of the story and saw David with his black eyes, Donald was not on their Christmas Card List.
The years at Bangor High School passed day by day, week by week, month by month and year by year. Donald did not truly excel in the academic arena, and was unsure on the actual reason. Was it that he was just thick, was it because of his environment, was it because

as like his siblings, he was kept in the dark and fed poop. Whatever the reason, Donald had one thing that most teenagers seemed to lack, and that was self-belief, confidence and a flair for bullshit.

Donald had great ambitions, and dreamed one day that he would become Prime Minister! If that is not ambitious, what is? He enjoyed reading the TIME magazine, as he had an avid interest in politics and current affairs. In January 1965 when Sir Winston Churchill died. Donald bought a souvenir magazine of the great man for the grand sum of five shillings, keeping it as a family heirloom. Donald also bought a copy of 'The Politics of Hate' in 1968 which commemorated the assassination of Senator Robert Kennedy.

When it came to the Certificate of Secondary Education, Donald did not do too well. The only subject that he achieved an A Grade was Art. He was unable to study History for CSE exams as the subject was dropped due to a lack of interest with Donald's class mates.

Donald's sister Elsie was trundling along without any major disasters. Nanna Fanny doted on Elsie, and pampered Elsie as much as she could.

CHAPTER FOUR
LIFE AFTER SCHOOL

Donald's brother Ronald had left school a year earlier than Donald. Mr Cossak at the newsagents had offered his paper boy of the year an upgrade to shop assistant at his shop. Ronald readily accepted, and Mr Cossak paid Ronald a £5.00 a week salary.

When it came for Donald to hang up his paper round bag and look for employment, Mr Cossack also offered Donald a position in the same shop. He assured Donald that he himself would not be his boss, but his brother Ronald would be instead. This was supposed to reassure Donald, but in fact it had the opposite effect. Donald had no ambition to work in the same shop as his brother, and certainly not allow Ronald to Lord it over him, especially when he had endured sixteen years of subservience.

Instead Donald found a position as porter in 'The Brown Cow' Hotel on the other-side of Bangor. The role involved cleaning the lounges, hotel bar, making up the coal fires and serving afternoon teas.
The wage was £8.00 per week plus tips. Donald found that he was averaging £10.00 a week with tips.

Donald got stuck into the work at the Hotel which was part of the Trust House Forte Group. Mr & Mrs Starfitt where the managers. Mr Starfitt was English and Mrs Starfitt was a stunningly beautiful black and elegant South African lady. Mr & Mrs Starfitt were kind to Donald, and pleased that he carried out his duties with quiet aplomb.
The cost of a Full Afternoon Tea comprising of various sandwiches, cakes, biscuits and tea served in Silver Teapots was Four Shillings and Sixpence. The teas were taken in the expansive lounge and was indeed a grand affair. Donald did quite well for tips. One day he received a full four shillings and sixpence as a tip from just one customer.

In the hotel kitchen, the head cook was a middle aged woman called Ellen. She was hard-working and cooked meals of the highest standard. The Head waiter was a skinny young man called Harold. He looked smart in his flash red jacket, black dickie bow tie, and black trousers with a black silk strip down the outside of each leg. The washer-up man was a middle-aged, obese, balding guy called Bob, who had learning difficulties. He lodged at the hotel in a small staffroom. He was not a friendly man by nature, and when he saw Donald coming and going from the kitchen, he would give him a baleful look.
Donald would sometime have to work late into the evenings at the hotel, serving suppers to residents with room service. So he had to visit the kitchen. Unbeknown to Donald, washer upper Bob had a melt-down, and the managers were notified. Bob told them that it was seeing Donald at the hotel that was disturbing him. Mr & Mrs Starfitt asked Donald to come into the office, and they explained

Bob's melt down, and that he was the main reason. Donald asked what the solution may be, and the Starfitts said "Well try and keep out of his way!" It was left like that, and Donald wondered how he could comply with that instruction as he worked at the hotel. The good news was that Bob did not have any further melt downs.

It was coming up to Christmas at the hotel, and a staff party had been arranged. Although Donald was only sixteen and had never drank alcohol, he was taken to various pubs with other staff, celebrating the approach to Christmas. Donald thought he would try a tot of Queen Anne Scotch Whisky, and although it burnt his throat, he had another, and another, until he lost count and nearly lost consciousness. After around two hours of bonhomie, Donald decided it was time to stagger home, so departed the throng, and no one noticed his departure. With one eye closed and the other squinting, Donald trundled down town. Feeling hot and bilious, he decided to lie down flat out on the pavement, feeling the cold penetrating his raincoat, and cooling him quickly. Donald woke to find that he had stretched out on the pavement outside the Police Station, and nobody had noticed the body on the pavement. He staggered to his feet, and carried on in the direction of home. He tried to be as quiet as possible, as he navigated the stairs. Not quite enough, as when he got to the bedroom door, his father yelled from the other bedroom "Is that you Donald? Are you drunk?" Donald slurred "No I just had two glasses of sherry!" With that he slunk into the bedroom where Ronald was sound asleep.

During this period Ronald asked Donald if he would bring back some miniature bottles of whisky for him from the hotel. Donald brought back four bottles, and watched as Ronald, who had seen cowboys on the Western movies slugging back shots of whisky with great ease. He drank the four bottles in four gulps, the effect was really quite fast. Ronald's eyes began to glaze, and his colouring changed from fleshy to red to a nasty shade of eau de nil, he then threw up onto the bedroom floor. Ronald vowed never to touch whisky again in his entire life.

It was during the nine months at the Hotel that Ellen the Cook spoke to Donald, and said that the best job for him, would be to go to sea. "Join the Merchant Navy and see the World!" she said.

Donald asked her if she had been to sea, and she said that he had not, but had heard that it was a good career. This intrigued Donald, so he made enquiries on what he had to do to 'go to sea.'

Donald found that the Merchant Navy were recruiting Catering and Deck Boys at the Liverpool Shipping Federation which was located on Mann Island in Liverpool. Donald told his father that he wanted to join the Merchant Navy. Walter was not too happy with that idea and told Donald just to carry on with the job he already had. Donald ignored this advice, and applied for an interview with the Liverpool Federation. This building was known as the Pool, where for the North-West of England, seafarers could look at what was on the board, see what ships were in Liverpool, and what ratings where required for trips away at sea.

Donald took a bus from Bangor to Liverpool and turned up for his interview. He sat in a chair opposite a man behind a desk, who eyed Donald up and down, and flicked his eyes back to the application form. Donald was dressed in a nice blazer, with a collar and tie, as he wanted to be smart for his interview.

The interview was short, and after a few preliminary questions. The man looked quizzically at Donald, and said "Are you really sure that you want to go to sea? It can be a hostile environment."
Donald replied yes indeed that he wanted to join todays Merchant Navy. After all Ellen, the Cook had recommended the career, even though she knew nothing about going to sea. The interviewer then told Donald that he could rise through the ranks and become a Catering Officer. This sounded good enough for Donald. He attended a medical examination after the interview, and was told that the Federation would be in touch with him in due course, and subject to the results of the medical, he would be attending a ten week course at the sea-school at Gravesend, Kent.

Donald passed the medical with flying colours, and within two weeks was enrolled on the Gravesend Sea-School course. Donald's parents weren't fazed either way with events, and Donald was pleased that he had made his own decision to change the course of his life.

Donald travelled by train from Bangor to Euston and then a connecting train down to Gravesend in Kent. The future seemed daunting, but was also exciting. The new intake of around 40 boys were each given a uniform, consisting of a short tunic, white shirt, black tie and black trousers and shoes, topped off with a beret. They were allocated to various dormitories, and there were around 20 boys to each dormitory. All the dormitories were named after various passenger liners.

Roll call was every morning, and the boys in each class had been allocated an instructor who taught them how to stand to attention, about turn, stand at ease, a little like any military force. The boys ate their food in a large hall with long tables. Donald thought that the food was brilliant. It was hot, and there were servings of meat and lots of vegetables. A steward used to slam down an aluminium jug of ready-made tea (milk and sugar already added). There was a lot of grumbling about the food from many of the newcomers, and Donald was bemused at to what they had to moan about. This was food that was fit for the gods, in his opinion.

Within a fortnight, Donald was promoted to the position of a Leading Hand, he was given a lanyard which could be looped through one of the lapels on the shoulder, and a sew-on badge with crossed anchors. It was not clear why Donald was chosen to be a Leading Hand, the reason was more likely to Donald's height. He was a strapping 6ft 2" lad. Donald was now Dormitory lead in being responsible for maintaining good behaviour and his troupe obeying all Instructors orders. Basically the responsibilities of an NCO.

The ten weeks sped by, and Donald learned all that there was to know about the rudiments of basic catering, and what to expect on-board a vessel at sea. Donald was issued with a certificate of competency and left the sea-school.

On his way back on the train at Euston Station, he found it difficult to find a seat in any of the carriages. All the passengers were squeezed in and they seemed to be piled up onto each other. Donald noticed a carriage with only one very old gent who was sleeping, and thought this is a great find. So he settled comfortably into one of the many empty seats, and looked through the glass at the other carriage with all those people piled on each other. They glared sullenly back at Donald. He just could not understand why they did not want to spread out a little. The journey was very comfortable from Euston Station to Bangor, and it was only when Donald was alighting the coach at Bangor that he noticed a large '1' on the carriage glass door, and written underneath were the words 'First Class' Oops!

Donald returned home to await the call for when a ship required crewing and wanted a catering boy.
A letter arrived with written instruction that Donald was to be appointed as Catering Boy on-board an iron ore carrier, called 'IRON BARQUE', registered in Newcastle. The vessel would be alongside at Gladstone Dock, Liverpool. A rail warrant was included with the letter, and Donald set off for his first sea-going adventure. He arrived in Liverpool with one very large ungainly heavy suitcase. Donald only had a vague idea on the location of the vessel but was surprised how long it took to walk to Gladstone Docks, especially with a suitcase that was getting heavier all the time. After around and hour and a half, and two miles later, he arrived at the foot of the gangway leading to the IRON BARQUE.
Donald proceeded up the gangway with his suitcase. Unsure where to go, he wondered into an alleyway, with doors on one side. It looked dark and dingy, as the bulkheads were a dirty grey colour and pipework lined the bulkheads. Donald spotted some stairs and walked up the stairs. The décor improved the further he climbed, and the bulkheads were now oak, and there were framed prints adorning the bulkheads. This was much better, thought Donald. He was met at the top of the stairs by a man in a white shirt, gold and silver epaulettes, black tie, and trousers. He asked if Donald was one of the new catering boys. Donald answered in the affirmative. The man introduced himself as the Purser, he then went into his office and picked up the phone and talked to someone. Within a minute, a young skinny man with a pencil moustache, who looked like a Mexican, but was actually a Geordie, turned up. He asked Donald to follow him, and both he and Donald went back down the stairs. Back down to the dingy alleyway where Donald had already been. Mr Moustache opened a cabin door that was located beneath the stairs and told Donald that this was his cabin. Donald went into the cabin which measured around 8ft x 8ft, and saw two metal bunks on one side of the cabin, and a single metal bunk on

the other side. There was a chest of 3 drawers, and 3 small metal lockers.

Donald proceeded to unpack. He then went to explore, and found the galley. He met the Chief Cook who was a black Jamaican middle aged man. The man told Donald that he would be the Galley Boy and that he would be sharing the cabin with the pantry boy, and the mess boy. Donald soon realised that the new pantry boy had been a friend in his class at the sea-school, a ginger curly haired lad called Roger Brake. Donald was pleased that he knew somebody that he would be sailing with.

That night the vessel departed Liverpool and was to load iron ore at Lulea, in Sweden. As the vessel steamed out of the Mersey, Donald and Roger hung their heads out of the portholes, looking at all the bright port lights and both were excited as to what the future held. The deck crew laughed at the boys, and told them to get their heads in as it was not a cattle ship.

The next day the weather was breezy as the ship travelled north heading for Scotland. Donald got to grips being a galley boy, and was busy washing up pots and pans. Peeling potatoes and vegetables, cleaning the cooking range and all the other cleaning duties.

The further north the ship travelled, the choppier the seas became. It was not before long that Roger was being violently sick. The Chief Cook found this amusing, and said that he had the better boy, as Donald was not being sick (yet). It was not long after, that Donald felt really unwell, the ship was lurching from side to side, and then slamming down with a shudder. The weather, now that the ship had past the coast of Scotland had become much worse. Donald lay on his bunk, and wished that he could go to sleep and die peacefully. Anything to stop feeling so wretched. He still had to wash the pots in the galley sink, feeling really miserable. Looking at the greasy water in the galley sink, slopping from side to side was making Donald feel bilious. The Chief Cook and Second Cook had no sympathy for Donald. The Chief Cook told Donald "Buck up and 'get your tits over that sink!"

After a violent night, the weather improved the next day, and the sea was calmer. Roger and Donald felt immediately a lot better.

One morning when Donald was busy washing the pots and pans. The weather was warm, so he was wearing a T shirt, shorts, socks and shoes. The Cook was clearing up after the Breakfast serving and Donald had not noticed that the Chief Cook had lifted a large frying pan with hot oil from the range and placing it directly under the galley sink. Donald returned to the sink, and his foot caught on the long handle of the frying pan, which then flipped up and the hot oil poured onto Donald's shin, collecting around the sock. The pain was excruciating and Donald's leg had become bright red and was swelling quickly. Donald did not want to make a fuss, and did his best to keep the wound clean, to cause as little disruption as possible. The wound became increasingly worse. It was during this time that the Purser decided to swap the galley boy and pantry boy around. Donald became the pantry boy, and Roger became the galley boy. Donald was now responsible for cleaning officers' cabins, along with the Purser's cabin. All the Officers cabins were sumptuous in comparison to the ratings cabins. All the Officers even had their own en-suite bathrooms.

Donald was cleaning the Purser's cabin one day, whilst the Purser was sat at his desk. When Donald had finished the cabin, he started to make for the door. The Purser called to him, and said "Donald, please can you hoover my carpet?" "But I only hoovered it the day before yesterday" responded Donald. "Yes, but I would like it hoovered everyday please" the Purser informed him. "Every day! My mother only hoovers once a week" explained Donald. "Well you can hoover my carpet every day! If you don't mind" said the Purser.

The burn to Donald's leg was becoming really painful, and it was not healing. Donald had noticed that the Purser had some antibiotic cream in his bathroom cabinet, so he used some of the cream on his leg in the hope that the infection would clear up. It didn't, and it just got worse. In the end Donald showed the injury to the Purser, so that when the ship berthed in Cardiff, Donald was given the address of a doctor, as an appointment had been made for him to attend a surgery. Donald had to walk for two miles to the surgery, limping in pain all the way. Upon inspection at the surgery, the doctor was appalled at the sight of the injury, and prescribed antibiotics to clear the infection. He also sent a note to the ship to advise that Donald should sign off immediately and be repatriated home for convalescence.

So this was the course of action taken. Donald's trip had lasted 2.5 months, and as the pay was £24.00 a month. Donald was pleased to receive the princely wage of over £60.00.

Donald returned home to Bangor to await his next ship. Three weeks later, he was instructed to travel to Liverpool to join the Shell Tanker, SS Hinnites. A small product tanker. Donald travelled to Liverpool and joined the ship signing on for a 6 months trip.

He joined the vessel as Pantry Boy, and was going up in the world, as this ship had single berth cabins, so he had his own space. Donald signed a company contract with Shell Tankers (UK) Ltd, which meant that he would only join Shell vessels. This worked well for Donald, as he craved a sense of familiarity, a commitment to one company with a clear path for promotion.

During his time on-board the Hinnites, Donald was now 17 years old. He was still a cherry boy, meaning still a virgin. The ship used to coast to various ports within the United Kingdom, and one of these ports was a Scottish town called Ardrossan, a town on the North Ayrshire coast, in southwestern Scotland.

The crew were granted shore-leave, and Donald went with a few of his shipmates ashore one evening. After calling at a few pubs in the town, they came across three ladies. Well ladies of the night. They certainly were not young girls, but progressing more into the middle age bracket. After treating these ladies to a few drinks, it was decided to bring the 'girls' back to the ship. Donald was paired up with a small woman, with ample bosoms and plenty of make-up. Donald escorted her to his cabin which was situated aft of the vessel. (The ship had two accommodation blocks, one amid ships, and the other aft of the vessel. Both accommodation blocks were linked by a 'flying bridge' which is a bridge that stands over the deck pipe work on the main deck).

As this was Donald's first time in the bedroom department, he thought that it would be quite enjoyable. However, after much fumbling, kissing and the like. The woman asked Donald "Have you done this before?" To which Donald replied "Yes on many occasions!" Donald eventually got around to completing the initiation, but felt totally underwhelmed. Hopefully things would improve. During the association, Donald kept thinking that this lady was as near as damn it as old as his mother, Margo. When it came to paying this lady for her services, Donald did not have any money, and it was agreed that she would have his new transistor radio, which Donald had paid a full £11.00. The woman left Donald dressed in only a towel, and upon letting her out of the cabin, and showing her out of the alleyway. A draught from an outside door slammed closed his cabin door which was on a Yale lock. So Donald was now locked out of his cabin. He then had to go out of the accommodation block and along the Flying Bridge to see the Duty Officer and ask for the Master key so that he could get back into his cabin.

Donald remembered what the initial interviewer said when he first visited the Liverpool Federation when he first applied to join the British Merchant Navy. The interviewer had asked if Donald really wanted to go to sea. As Donald was a rating that was relatively naive when it came to other young people in general. During the 1960's the British Merchant Navy had a fleet of over two thousand vessels, so crewing them was a monumental task, and not everyone wanted a career at sea away from their families for long periods of time. So there were many down and out characters, sometimes homeless, who would join the Merchant Navy. Donald met many that were alcoholics, drug addicts, thugs and people with no scruples whatsoever. However, there were many decent people who were actually the salt of the earth, but to be honest there were equal measures of the good and the bad, and even the downright ugly!

As many did not have any goals and ambition, they were also loathe to see someone else succeed, so Donald felt at times really lonely, as when he joined the crowd in the evening at the crew bar, free flowing alcohol would bring out the worst in some people, and violence would ensue, where on one occasion the fridge was ripped from its anchorage and tossed overboard into the sea.

Donald would spend the evening reading books, or playing chess. Long trips at sea, meant very limited shore leave, so crew would have to look for as much as possible to entertain themselves and stop the boredom. A similar situation like the lockdown brought about by the coronavirus.

Donald was learning so much more about people and life since he had joined the Navy. He found it easy to analyse people, and the close proximity of people working and living together made it simple to understand the person within. In usual circumstances, people can hide their true characters behind a façade of respectability, and many people are able to fool other people all of the time. It is more difficult to sustain a façade on-board a cramped vessel for months on end.

After three vessels serving as Catering Boy, Donald was promoted to the rank of Assistant Steward. This work involved cleaning Officers cabins and serving at tables in the Officers Dining Saloon. In those days, there was silver service and officers enjoyed relatively high cuisine consisting of three courses.

Donald was a mediocre Assistant Steward as he was not hugely keen on cleaning cabins. Most times, he would enter a cabin to clean it, and see a magazine or book lying on the officer's desk, and he would proceed to read it. The time would pass quickly, before Donald then realised that he has to get on, so he would straighten the sheets and pillows, rub some vim around the sink, and then move on to the next cabin.

News came that Grandad Archibald had passed away suddenly. He was 78 years old. He had developed pneumonia and died in hospital. Donald liked Grandad Archibald, though he knew that Archibald preferred Ronald to him. Once as teenagers, when it was Grandad Archibald's birthday, Ronald had bought him 10 Woodbine cigarettes, and Donald managed to scrape up enough money to buy him 20 Players cigarettes which were a better quality tobacco and more expensive. Grandad Archibald made a great deal more fuss over the Woodbines than he did with the Players Cigarettes. It just shows that money can't buy love!

It was during this time as Assistant Steward that Donald travelled to a vessel called the ALINDA. He made friends with lads of his age, and struck up a friendship with a Deck Cadet called Stephen Briggs. Deck Cadets were trainee officers. They had a good relationship, and they went shore together, played chess and enjoyed each other's company. Donald lent Stephen a radio, as Stephen did not have any form of a music outlet, whilst Donald had a tape recorder and also a radio.

So after some time, it was with great disappointment that Donald had found that Stephen no longer had the radio in his possession, in fact he had sold it to somebody ashore. Not really the honest thing to do, especially when the radio was not his to sell.

Not knowing how he could rectify this injustice. Donald went to see the Master of the vessel, who was Captain William Miller. Donald explained the situation to the Captain. The advice from Captain Miller was that he could not do anything about it personally, but that Donald should thrash if out physically with Stephen Briggs. Donald interpreted that he should give Stephen a good thump around the ear. So he went down to Stephen's cabin, knocked on the door and opened it to see Stephen sitting at his desk. He reiterated the advice of the Master and called Stephen out onto the deck. After a few feints from both parties, fists collided between the two protagonists'. After much thumping by both parties, Donald eventually stopped due to breathlessness. Shook hands, and Donald left the scene of conflict. All done and dusted, and no loss of face.

Following two ships as Assistant Steward, Donald was promoted to Second Cook and Baker. He had no idea about cooking. Which was just as well, as the company would pay for a six week course at the Nautical Catering College in Liverpool. Douglas attended the college, kitted out into a chef's uniform complete with *Toque*. When Donald walked out of the changing room dressed in his fancy dress, he hoped that no one would ask him to make a pan of custard, as he would not have had a clue at all.

The class was split into two groups, the ones with cooking experience, and the one's without any experience. Donald joined the latter group.

Donald enjoyed the cooking course, learning how to bake bread, pastries, biscuits and cakes. The preparation and cooking of meats, pies, vegetables. Learning all about the theory of catering and good housekeeping, together with kitchen hygiene.

At the end of the course there were practical and theory examinations, and Donald was overall top of the class in both theory and practical exams.

Donald's first trip as a Second Cook & Baker was a challenge. The Chief Cook was a bully and lacked patience. When Donald was trying to crack eggs against the frying pan, the Chief Cook used to press his hand down into the oil which caused burns to his knuckles. Donald was in the rank of 2nd Cook & Baker for a period of two years. During that time, Donald met some Chief Cooks that were good and a couple of Chief Cooks that were totally in the wrong job, with no cooking ability whatsoever. However, he learned quickly and became a competent 2nd Cook.

As there were few people available on ship who could cut hair. Donald bought himself a pair of hair clippers, thinning scissors, combs and a cut throat razor. He would then cut hair for all the ratings, and sometimes an officer, who were in dire need of a trim. As there were times that a lack of shore leave meant insufficient time to visit a professional barber. The crew appreciated his hair cutting skills. Well, nobody complained, so that was good enough in itself. As he also enjoyed art work, he would sketch pictures for crew members of any subject that they liked, and they would adorn their cabin bulkheads with the pictures.

Donald travelled the world and he enjoyed visiting many countries and especially liked the Caribbean and South America. Dutch Shell owns a large refinery on an island in the Caribbean called Curacao. This was a friendly island and part of the Dutch Antilles. The people were friendly and many Shell Tankers visited the port along with other ships of various nationalities. In order that the many seafarers who visited the island were sure to enjoy themselves whilst they were ashore. There was a complex that had once been a military barracks, and then transformed into a giant nightclub, with the barracks rented to beautiful South American girls with olive brown skin and stunning beauty. Whether they were Venezuelan, Brazilian, Argentinian, they were all gorgeous, and had learned their public relations skills to a very high standard. Everyone enjoyed their time at what was known as Campo Allegro.

Whilst serving on-board the SS Hindsia in the Far East in 1973, orders were received from London that the ship would call at the port of Saigon, South Vietnam. The Vietnam War going at full throttle at that time, with North Vietnamese forces putting pressure on the South Vietnamese forces, who were supported by the United States, and were fully involved with supporting the South Vietnamese government with their own armed forces fighting alongside the South Vietnamese troops.

Donald and crew were heading for a war zone, and no one on-board at that time was particularly fazed at the prospect, in fact it was viewed as more of an adventure than anything else. As the vessel approached the port of Saigon, black plumes of smoke could be seen billowing into the sky from a recent raid on an oil refinery near the city. The vessel docked successfully. South Vietnamese soldiers boarded the vessel, and from time to time, they threw grenades into the water surrounding the vessel. This was to deter the Vietcong using divers to plant bombs to the hull of the vessel. This strategy did not work, as the Vietcong did indeed manage to send divers down, and they had attached a limpet mine to the stern of the vessel just as the ship was leaving port. The 'clang' on the hull was heard from the engine-room steering flat, and the incident reported to the bridge. The Master turned the ship around and headed back to port. The hull was inspected by South Vietnamese Navy divers and there they found evidence that a mine had indeed been attached, though it had not detonated successfully.

Other Shell Tankers during the Vietnamese war were not so fortunate, one vessel suffered rocket propelled damage to the accommodation and some of the seafarers suffered from shrapnel wounds and burns.

It was during this period that Donald saw a lot of the Far East. In those days, the Far East was still a place of mystery and adventure. Donald had visited Singapore on many occasions. Singapore was beginning its boom as a service industry to the world. It was an ideally situated island that was once just humid marshland, and was now becoming a booming economy. In those days there were still seamy places for sailors to visit. Anson Road was a great place with eating houses, bars, strip joints and gorgeous ladies of the night. The night life was tremendous with loud music booming out of the various bars.

Bugi Street was another tourist location, eating houses lined both sides of the street. Also well known for its Kai Tai's, these were young male transvestite escorts who walked in stiletto heels, luxurious bouffant wigs, wearing lurid face make up with eye shadow and lipstick. The boys did indeed look like glamorous girls. The Kai Tai's in those days were organised by an Australian Sergeant Major, who ensured discipline and looked after the welfare of the young men.

Tourists could sit outside on the street amongst the many tables belonging to the various eating houses, and a little girl called Mary would approach the table and offer anyone a challenge to beat her at noughts and crosses. Whoever won, would win One Singapore Dollar. It was very rare indeed that Mary ever lost a game.

There was also a Chinese violinist who would come between the tables playing his violin and singing 'Santa Lucia'. In fact that appeared all that he could sing. Every time Donald was in Bugi Street on his many visits, Santa Lucia was still being sung to the continuous throng of tourists.

Donald began taking his leave in Singapore as Shell Tankers owns a small island off Singapore called Pulau Bukom. The island is a giant oil refinery, and many Shell Tankers called at Singapore. It was easy for Donald to work on-board a vessel for around 6 months and then take three to four weeks leave in Singapore. He would stay at the Seventh Storey Hotel in Rochore Road, which charged eight Singapore Dollars a night, which was around £1.50pence. During World War Two, the Seventh Storey Hotel was easily the best hotel in Singapore at that time. However in the late 1960's and early 1970's it had fallen well behind the swanky hotels that were now numerous in Singapore. The hotel did boast a noisy air conditioning system, so was relatively comfortable.

Donald was alone taking his leave from a vessel, he met many locals of Chinese origin of his own age. They would meet at the YMCA near Stamford Bridge, and go out in a group to watch Bruce Lee films, and visit the Hyatt Hotel which boasted a bowling alley. As Donald's Chinese friends were all involved in Martial Arts, Donald joined the Taekwondo classes. Donald was merely a white belt, and never progressed any further. It was at a Taekwondo class that he met with a German called Peter who joined the group. Whilst Peter and Donald were sparring, Donald kicked Peter in the shin, which did not hurt Peter, but Donald was in excruciating pain, and felt that he had broken his big toe. The toe swelled up to twice its size, and Donald's Chinese friends packed the toe in ice and towels. Donald then had to wear an open toed sandal for a fortnight, and he also gave up on the Taekwondo experiment.

When Donald needed some company in the evening, Singapore was a fine place to hire a prostitute for the night, and lovely Chinese girls would always be on hand to ensure that nights were not too long and dull.

Though, amongst the crowd of Chinese friends that Donald had befriended, he met a young Chinese girl of 20 years old called Suzanna, and her father was a financer, and wealthy man. The family were owners of a detached bungalow and very large gardens. Even in those days, land in Singapore was at a premium and for someone who owned a detached property with land was indeed hugely wealthy. Suzanna and Donald used to travel in rickshaws through the streets of Singapore, and Donald used to sing to this lovely girl, who was tickled pink to be serenaded by a young lunatic lad for Great Britain.

Suzanna was to hold her 21st Birthday celebration at one of Singapore's most prestigious hotels, but unfortunately Donald was away at sea, and could not make the occasion. The relationship fizzled out as life moved on.

Sad news was received, in that Grandpop Humphrey had passed away. He had been always been a workaholic and had been digging an inspection pit at the garage annexed to his home in the welsh mountains. He felt stabbing pains in his chest, which turned out to be a heart attack. Nanna Fanny called 999 and asked for an ambulance. The ambulance arrived, and the medics wanted to stretcher him into the ambulance, but Grandpop Humphrey insisted on walking to the vehicle. He called to Fanny and asked her to come to the hospital later and bring his shaving kit.

Grandpop Humphrey arrived at the hospital, but his condition deteriorated, and he died on the same day. Donald felt the impact of his death, as Grandpop Humphrey was his one and only ally in the family group, and had always been supportive of Donald. Grandpop Humphrey had bought a motor scooter for Donald, and was in the process of over-hauling the engine and giving it to

Donald. The world had lost a good man. Grandpop Humphrey was only 59 years old.

Grandpop Humphrey's death affected Nanna Fanny, but only inasmuch that she thought that it was impertinent of him to die before her, as she thought that their unwritten domestic contract was that he would be there for her until her own demise.

She was so angered about his premature death, that she went into the garage and kicked all the debris and cement bags into the unfinished inspection pit.

She then put the house up for sale, but as she was a poor business woman, with only limited capacity to think one day at a time. She snapped up the first ludicrous low offer of purchase from the first prospective buyer, selling the property that Grandpop Humphrey had put his heart into building for what he believed to be the love of his life. The property was sold for half of its value.

Nanna Fanny moved into Bangor town, and rented a two bed flat above the same newsagent's shop that Ronald and Donald had worked as newspaper boys. Nanna Fanny had bought a poodle called Kim and brought the dog up in a spoilt and improper manner, in that she only allowed the dog to drink milk rather than water. She thought that the dog would benefit from milk rather than water. Needless to say that Kim endured a short and miserable life, dying within three years.

Donald's sister Elsie moved into Nanna Fanny's flat as Elsie also worked as a shop assistant in the shop below. She was spoilt by Nanna Fanny who made her delicious meals and did her laundry, cleaned her bedroom and basically doted on her. Elsie developed Nanna Fanny's habits in being house proud, and everything had to be spick and span at all times.

At the age of 21 years old, Donald was promoted to the rank of Chief Cook. He attended another course at the Nautical Catering College in Liverpool and gained his part 2 certificate of cooking entitling him to sail in the rank of Chief Cook.

Donald was successful in the rank of Chief Cook at such an early age, and especially considering that just a few short years earlier, he had no idea about the production of food, menus and catering in general.

He was sailing on a super tanker during his period as Chief Cook. A super tanker is a vessel which in those days averaged over 200,000 tonnes. The ships were used on many occasions to sail to the Middle- East, to ports in the UAE, Iran, Iraq and Saudi Arabia for example. The ships' would sail to ports and load cargo many miles from the shore by long fuel lines, so that crew were unable to go ashore.

The ships then would sail back to Europe to ports such as Rotterdam, and discharge the cargo along similar pipe lines, many miles from shore. Sometimes, if a contract was for a period of six months, this meant that no shore leave at all for the full six months contract. Fresh provisions and fresh water were delivered by barge to the vessel.

It was on one of the VLCC ships that Donald was assigned, and as they were not popular vessels due to no shore leave, therefore they were much more difficult to crew. This meant that the company would have to resource ratings from the Shipping Federation. Donald found that he was the only contracted rating on-board the vessel, whilst all the other ratings including the Bosun, Deck Storekeeper, Pumpman, Engine-room Storekeeper, Firemen, AB's, Ordinary Seaman, 2nd Cook, 2nd Steward, Stewards, Pantry and Galley boys were all Shipping Federation crew.

This was indeed a motley crew, and they were the worst crowd of people on-board a ship that Donald had encountered. The Bosun was a complete drunken sot. The AB's were not interested in a day's work. The second cook was a long-haired, scruffy, unshaven young man, who happened to be an insomniac, up all night, and wanting to sleep all day when he should be working. The Chief Steward who was an Officer, was a frightened little man, who seemed scared of his own shadow, and certainly had no leadership qualities whatsoever. When Donald used to call at the Chief Steward's office each morning to discuss the following day's menu, this little man would scurry from his bathroom, wiping his hands in a towel. Donald soon realised that post of Chief Steward involved very little actual work, and this Chief Steward spent most of his time trying to avoid being seen, and therefore ducking out of any responsibilities at the drop of a hat. Donald had very little respect for this excuse of a man, as the Chief Steward did not support him in disciplining the second cook for being totally useless at his work, and was a health hazard to the crew in general, as the second cook had a very poor personal hygiene regime. He was the bread-maker, and his loaves of bread would appear out of the blue, sometimes out of his cabin. The bread was usually stale and solid. At times, he would leave the dough to prove and then disappear into his cabin, whilst the dough would rise and then escape from the Hobart machine and work its way along the deck of the galley becoming bigger and bigger like a great giant dollop of goo.

As the vessel was guaranteed no shore leave, and the route was the same throughout each trip. To load cargo at a port in the Middle East from a pipeline many miles from shore and back again to Rotterdam to discharge cargo from a similarly long pipe line. The trips were long and boring as the ship was too large to transit the Suez Canal, so had to go around the coast of Africa, passing the Cape of Good Hope, where barges would come out to the vessel, or helicopters from Cape Town delivering fresh provisions and deck & engine-room spares.

Long trips at sea means that all crew have to maintain strong mental well-being in order to stave off boredom, as beyond daily tasks there is very little distraction from tedium to keep minds active and positive. Officers would keep watch either on the bridge or in the engine-room. For engine-room crew there was always a lot of various work that demanded their full attention such as maintenance and on-going repairs to the engine plant. Whereas for Deck Officers there was much more tedium during their four hour watch period. As the ship was at sea for many weeks at a time, and the courses already plotted, the time keeping watch on the bridge proved challenging in staving off boredom. The position of the Captain who was Master of the vessel, was even more challenging, as his workload was even further reduced, as he never held a bridge watch, and struggled to find stimulus to keeping his mind occupied.

This was the case of Captain Brian Polroyd. He was a middle aged balding man of around 5ft 5 inches. He had 'little man' syndrome, and used his position of power to make up for his limited stature, and his lack of reasonable mental balance. This man used his Captaincy to cow both senior and junior officers, who were literally frightened of challenging any of Captain Polroyd's decisions.

Together with the unfortunate circumstance that Captain Polroyd had inherited ratings of inadequate professionalism, meant that Captain Polroyd was out of his depth in being a successful Master.

Considering that Donald was the only rating on-board the vessel who was contracted to the company, and therefore an asset due to being more committed to the company. Captain Polroyd soon made it known that Donald, the Chief Cook was his main adversary, and the Master concentrated more on the Chief Cook than anyone else on-board. This was not good news for Donald. Not only was his line manager Chief Steward Bob Watt an ineffective boss and a wimp of a man. Donald's Second Cook was a long haired unkempt insomniac and useless 2nd Cook. The 2nd Steward and his two Assistant Stewards were drunks. The Messman was evidently gay, and kept giving Donald the eye. In fact the Messman eventually settled into domestic bliss with one of the Assistant Steward's. The only good rating was the Galley Boy, who although was from the Shipping Federation, was a well brought up lad, who assisted in the Galley, and covered the deficiencies of the 2nd Cook.

For Donald, as Chief Cook, he was an important rating on any ship, and the food, especially good food, was vitally important in maintaining high morale on-board the vessel. So Donald did indeed have his work cut out in doing a good job that would please the majority of officers and ratings.

So it was with surprise when news came back to the Galley that the Master was not happy with the standard of cooking. One day Captain Polroyd walked into the Galley and confronted Donald directly, saying "When I come down to a meal, I look forward to a meal that I will enjoy! Unfortunately on each and every occasion, I am disappointed in the quality of the meal". Donald gave this a second or two thought, and responded "Captain, I would like you to come down to your meals, sit down and eat your food, then leave and return to your cabin without further ado!"

With that the Captain turned on his heel and left the Galley.

Every Sunday morning there would be a Captains Inspection which involved the Master and his senior staff including the Chief Steward, trooping through the accommodation, inspecting the cleanliness, and looking for anything that required repair and maintenance. The public places included the Officers Saloon, the crew messrooms, pantries, galley, and walk in fridges and freezers.

Every Saturday evening after the day's normal duties, the catering department would scrub, clean and polish everything in sight in readiness of the impending inspection. This was the case for Donald and the Galley Boy, as the 2nd Cook as usual was nowhere to be found.

So around 1100 hours on Sunday was the usual time for the Captain dressed in white shirt, white shorts and white gloves, and also wearing his Merchant Navy cap would march into the galley, followed by his retinue of senior officers and the diminutive Chief Steward Bob Watt. The Master would always find fault with the cleanliness of the galley, the cleanliness of the fridges and freezers. However, after many inspections involving the same negative responses from the Master, one Sunday in question, stood out against all the other Sundays.

Captain Polroyd strutted in as usual at around 1100 hours, he looked at everything in the galley and then disappeared down below to the fridges and freezers, his retinue following dutifully behind him. After 10 minutes, Captain Polroyd emerges up the stairs to the galley and walks up to Donald, and face to face says "Amazing!" This stunned Donald, who thought that the Master may have undergone a lobotomy since his last visit. The Master, then went on to say "Amazing, that this galley is still not clean, the fridges are dirty and it is all a complete mess!" This outburst stung Donald, who then retorted "Captain! This is not a museum, this is a working galley, meaning that we have to continue cooking and preparing the lunch while you conduct your inspection. If you don't like it, you can lump it, now if you don't mind I have a lunch to prepare!" The blood drained from the face of Captain Polroyd, and his senior staff looked on like startled pigeons. With a quick, about-face, Captain Polroyd marched out of the galley with his retinue scurrying behind him.

Thirty minutes later, Chief Steward Bob Watt appeared in the Galley. He went up to Donald and said "The Captain would like to see you in his office this evening at 1900 hours." "What for?" Donald said "Promotion?" Donald saw the departure of the Chief Steward, slamming the door behind him and fetching his heels a wallop.

That particular Sunday evening involved Donald making fish suppers served in newspaper to the officers and ratings as a special supper. This was done without any payment of overtime, and done just to keep the crew happy.

So when Donald and the Chief Steward turned up at the Captains office at 1900 hours for the scheduled 'chat.' Donald entered to see the Captain sat behind his desk. Donald and Bob Watt stood in front of his desk. The Captain opened the conversation to say how disappointed he was in Donald. Then the Chief Steward started to whiningly support Donald, who stopped him in his tracks, sayin, "I have enough on my plate, without your useless input!" Donald then said to the Captain "I struggle every day with carrying out my duties to a high standard. I am not supported by this Chief Steward, and have a staff of very poor quality, excluding the galley boy. In fact, I am carrying out Fish suppers without additional pay, in order to keep the crew happy." The Master sat, stunned into silence. So Donald carried on and said "Well, it looks like this conversation is going nowhere, in fact the situation seems to be going around and around. So if you don't mind, I am going now, as I have fish suppers to serve to the crew." With that, Donald turned around and left the Captain's office.

The following morning, the Chief Steward came into the galley, and said that the Master wanted to give Donald a bottle of whisky. This may be construed as ungracious on Donald's part, as sometimes his obstinacy and stubbornness could also be his undoing, rather than be seen as valiant and courageous. Donald said to the Chief Steward "Tell the Captain that he can stick the bottle of whisky up his arse!"
The only positive result of this entire debacle was that the Captain never bothered Douglas again. However, the Captain hold a grudge.

It was during this trip that due to anarchy reigning with the ratings on-board. The pantry department of 2nd Steward and two assistant stewards wanted power of their own, and as Chief Steward Bob Watt had never attempted to lead the catering department and continued his self-isolation in his cabin (probably cocooned in his bathroom, washing his hands).One Assistant Steward who was particularly belligerent attempted to hold sway over the entire department, including ownership of Chief Cook Donald Drinkwater. It was now time for Donald to act. He confronted the Assistant Steward and leading him into the crew messroom, Donald set about smacking this upstart around the head and face with the full power of his fists. The Assistant Steward was stunned with the ferocity of the attack upon his person, and ran to the nearest chair, holding it aloft and throwing it at Donald, who calmly caught the chair deftly in his hands, putting it down, and then going in for the kill. The Assistant Steward eventually wriggled free and ran screaming from the messroom. That was the end to that attempted insurrection. There was no more trouble from the pantry department.

Just before the end of the trip, and when crew can sign off the vessel to be replaced by another crew. It was appraisal time, and the end report would give an analysis of a person's ability, with career prospects.
Chief Steward Bob Watt, presented Donald with his paper appraisal, for him to peruse and sign accordingly. Donald noticed that he had not been recommended for promotion, and although Bob Watt had promised his recommendation earlier on into the trip. The recommendation was nowhere to be seen. So Donald raised this with the Chief Steward, who back-tracked and said he would amend the appraisal. Donald told him not to bother, as a recommendation from him wasn't worth the paper it was written on. Donald noticed the tick boxes, the ticks were in pencil rather than ink. This raised immediate suspicion with Donald, who realised that once he had signed the appraisal, the pencilled ticks could be erased from their positive position and relocated to the much more negative area when inked. So he instructed the Chief Steward to ink in the ticks and ink his positive comments. Donald then signed the appraisal accordingly.

Donald left the vessel by launch with some officers and ratings. During the trip ashore, an officer said how he thought that the way the Captain had treated Donald was appalling. Donald looked at the officer, and said "Does it really matter?" No one was brave enough to stop the tyranny of the Master, and therefore comments and belated condolences were of no real import.

During the leave that followed the departure from the vessel. Donald received a telephone call from a marine personnel officer at the Shell Tankers offices in London. Donald was asked why he had received a good report from the Chief Steward, and why the Master had put a very negative foot note at the bottom of his appraisal.

Sneaky Polroyd! Donald replied to the personnel officer, that he had ensured that the Chief Steward was made to ink in the tick boxes and erase the pencilled tick marks, otherwise he would also have received a negative report from his line manager.

Donald was thoroughly pissed off, and said to the personnel officer that he would visit their office in London, in person, and give a full account of the management of the vessel. This frightened the personnel officer, who attempted to pacify Donald, and said that he now fully understood the situation. Donald thought that the Personnel Officer had not expected the fall-out from Donald. He had presumed that he was well placed to give Donald a severe reprimand. That was a task that Donald had relieved him of.

Donald realised that it was not easy being Donald. But his father Walter, although unaware of the potential good that he had done to Donald at an early age, had indeed made him the man he was. Donald had no intention of wimping out if any situation. No more bullying by anyone. Bullies have to be tackled as they should not be able run amok and destroy other peoples' lives just for their own gratification.

CHAPTER FIVE
LIFE AS A CATERING OFFICER

In 1975 Donald was promoted to the rank of Chief Steward at the tender age of twenty five. He was the youngest ever in history to have achieved this position within the company. Donald was well pleased with this accomplishment.

Before any assignment to the position of Chief Steward/Catering Officer, he had to attend the Nautical Catering College at Liverpool to undertake the Head of Department Course along with the Ships Captains Medical Course. As in the rank of Catering Officer, Donald would also be the ships medical officer. The course lasted a full six weeks, and Donald passed the Head of Department Course with flying colours. He did even better at the Ships Captains Medical Course as he came top of the class in the examination.

Donald always enjoyed the course work, as he had a very good memory and could easily retain information. He was far more accomplished than he had ever been at school, and seemed to blossom to becoming more of an academic than he had ever been.

It was a relief not to be living at home which in Donald's mind was a sterile and barren desert, where nothing much grew.

Life at sea for the first nine years had not been easy, although Donald had never considered himself to be better than anyone else, and never saw himself as a snob, he did find the climb from catering Boy to Catering Officer a long haul. There were fellow ratings who because they had no ambition or career goals, were also loath to see others achieve. Donald realised he did not want to be a rating for the rest of his life, so achieving Officer Status was the way to go. The Chief Steward/Catering Officer position was in Donald's opinion, a good rank, if utilised wisely it could be a very influential position, as the Catering Officer's line manager was the Master himself. The Catering Officer was after all, head of department. The Catering Officer's duties included managing the catering department. Being in charge of the catering budget and the ordering of provisions with ship chandlers. Running the on-board shop and bonded stores and catering hardware store. Looking after and keeping stock of the Officers bar. Dealing with customs and port officials. Compiling crew lists, completing victualling records which showed the costs of feeding a man per day within the company guidelines. Also responsible for first aid and medical emergencies. The dispensing of drugs from the medical locker, keeping a log of all drugs used and the medical attendance to Officers and Ratings.

Donald joined the MS Mena which was a Shell Tanker, crewed with Shell Officers, though the ship had been sold to the Thai Ocean Transport Company, as TOTCO wanted to crew the vessel eventually, with Thai Officers and ratings. For now the ship consisted of British Officers and a Filipino crew. Donald's accommodation consisted of an office, and then an adjoining day room, through to a bathroom. The medical locker was immediately in the same alleyway. Splendid accommodation in comparison to Donald's first trip as catering boy on the IRON BARQUE.

For Donald, the role as Catering Officer was indeed far better than that of Chief Cook. In the rank of Catering Officer, he was front of house, visible, and able to use his personality for the benefit of achieving respect both for himself and also for the entire catering department. Donald wanted catering on-board to be a combination of healthy food, variation, and something for all crew to look forward to when it came to mealtimes. Thanks to the fact that Donald had a vivid imagination, and able to invent an interest to the lunchtime and dinner menus, he devised at least one special dish of the day, and include some information about the special dish to the crew. So he thought up the 'Red Spot' where he looked through various recipes and introduced them into the menu, putting a red spot by the side of the dish on the menu. The red spot would then explain the origin of the dish with a short story that was mainly true, but then ran into the fictitious, and frankly at times, into the ludicrous. However, the red spot dishes became instantly popular inasmuch that they helped to break the tedium of the day, and both officers and ratings would look forward to meal times to see what the Catering Officer had dreamed up, and the story telling involved.

It was during this particular trip that Donald and the radio officer became good friends. The radio officer was a bespectacled young man called Dave Larkes. He was an unprepossessing young man, who looked like a brainy nerd, but was in fact a really clever guy, who like Donald, was a unique individual. As the saying goes 'Birds of a feather flock together'. Dave as Radio Officer, was akin the rank of Catering Officer, as they shared the same line manager who was the Captain. Dave would sit in his radio shack and tap away on his Morse code button sending out telegrams on a daily basis. To fulfil his sometimes boring duties, Dave would whittle away pieces of wood with his wood carving kit and make decorative 'Love Spoons'. They were really very good, as they were ornate and very cleverly carved. He also enjoyed embroidering pictures onto plain canvas from inside the radio shack.

He was always upbeat, and level headed, he was very good company for Donald, he posed no threat, and did not play politics of any dimension.

Donald and Dave would play games of chess and table tennis, and no matter how hard Donald tried, Dave always beat him at any game. For a chap who looked nerdy, he was very proficient!

When the vessel called at Sriracha (Si Racha) a town around 78 km from Bangkok in Thailand and close to Pattaya Beach. Everyone was excited to going ashore and seeking the pleasure that this port had to offer. However, in those days in the 1970's there were little restrictions and scant security for people boarding a ship in port. As Thailand is noted for beautiful people, especially the young ladies, there were an ample amount of young women available to come on-board and apply for temporary adoption for as long as the ship stayed in port. This suited both Donald and his friend Dave, who met two delightful young girls who offered to act as laundry maids, chambermaids and keep the lucky sailor's bed warm at night. Dave had chosen a gorgeous young girl with long wavy black hair and petite features. Whilst Donald had also chosen a sweet girl with short black hair, a terrific tight lipped smile. However, he failed to notice that when this young lass opened her mouth, her two top front teeth were missing. The gap was so wide, that you could have wedged a fat Havana cigar in-between the gap quite snugly.

Notwithstanding the gap, she was good company and the group would go ashore together as a foursome. Donald really liked Dave's young lady and suggested a swap. Donald's young lady heard of this proposal, and scolded Donald for being a 'Butterfly', and not to go from cabbage to cabbage! So Donald resigned himself to sticking with what he had.

All four trooped off to Pattaya Beach for an afternoon of sunshine. Dave noticed that there were Jet Ski's available for hire and proposed that he and Donald hired one each. A great time was had by weaving in and out narrowly missing each other, but as Dave was long sighted and was not wearing his spectacles, he misjudged Donald's speedy approach and steered in front of Donald's on-coming Jet Ski. Donald's craft hit Dave Ski amidships and Donald fell off the ski into the water whilst his jet ski somersaulted and landed inches from his head with the propeller still whirling. The engine housing had fallen off and quickly sank below the waves.

Upon reaching shore with what was left of the jet-ski. Donald and Dave were met by the rental owners who learning that the engine housing was missing, insisted that both young men, including the two girls get into the back of their truck and go to their offices. This turned out to be a scam, as the engine housing was likely to be retrieved without much ado or expense, and the rental company should really have had insurance in place to cover loss or damage. However, Donald and Dave were charged US$70.00 for the loss of the engine housing. In order to settle the situation quickly, they paid up, and put it all down to life's little challenges.

It is important for any seafarer, that they are equipped with interpersonal skills, as living in a tin box with twenty to thirty individuals requires, patience and tact, and the ability to work together, living together for up to six months at a time.

Not everyone likes everybody else, but you have to do the best that you can to be sociable, as harmony is much easier than conflict. Sometimes, harmony cannot always be achieved. For instance, one Chief Officer who was born and bred in Rhodesia (Zimbabwe) was sailing on the same ship as Donald, and at the beginning of the trip the two were amicable, but as the trip wore on the Chief Officer came to despise Donald, and needled him on many occasions. Donald, as usual, put up with the hassle while he ascertained the best way to deal with the situation. Donald ate his meals not in the Officers Saloon, but with the Galley Staff in the Galley or messroom. Purely because he could see more of the catering service from outside of the Saloon. The Chief Officer would ask if Donald thought that he was too good for him to eat with them in the Officers Saloon. Donald would look at him and say "If the cap fits, wear it!" The disdain in the Chief Officers eyes were a picture. It was as if he was wanting to punch the smug smile from Donald's face. Donald knew that he had one of those faces that people wanted to belt into next week. But he would laughingly tell people, that they would have to get in the queue, and that it was a very long queue. The Captain knew that the Chief Officer and Donald did not like each other, and when there was no news with regard to any recent confrontation between the pair, the Master thought then that all was well. So one day he said to Donald "You and the Chief Officer seem to be getting along better these day?" Donald agreed with the Captain. "Never better!" he said "The reason, we get along so well, is that he stays out of my way, and I stay out of his!"

When the Falklands war was in full swing. Donald was selected, along with his friend Captain John Foot to join the EBALINA in the Royal Navy base at Rosyth, and the ship would sail to Ascension Island and supply fuel to the war machine currently taking place in the Falklands Islands. However, the war was over before the vessel could reach its destination.

Captain Foot was the Master, with a Chief Engineer Paddy O'Leary from Dublin, and a Chief Officer, called Gary Turbott from Essex. They turned out to be the gang of three. They wanted Donald to opt in and make it the gang of four. Donald realised that if he made up the number, then it would be detrimental to the management of the catering department, as he realised that the Chief Engineer and Chief Officer wanted Donald only as a junior partner and not a full partner. In Donald's view, he was not going to be held to ransom by three gangsters. So he declined the invitation, which then made him a target, and they considered that as they were three against one, they were odds on to be the winners. Pity that they had not reckoned with Donald's fortitude.

Chief Engineer Paddy O'Leary was the ring leader, and his ego knew no bounds. He considered himself to be way above mere mortals, and would make as much trouble as he could, just because of his rank and the power to be troublesome. He was as two-faced as a kipper, who like the smiling assassin, would say to Donald "Well, what fine fare do we have on the menu today?" Donald would tell him what was on the menu. Then Paddy would spread his hands expansively and say "Mmmm, every meal a banquet!" He was a cheeky sod, as information from my steward in the dining saloon would inform me that he was making trouble again at the table and running down the quality of the food and what was on the menu. The standoff lasted for four months, there was no quarter given on either side, though Donald could see that the gang of three were tiring, as they had not achieved Donald's surrender. The trip was nearing its end, and Paddy would turn up at Donald's office and ask from the door "When are we going to make an end?" Donald would smile and answer "When I've finished!" The Gang of Three now wished they had never started the vendetta, they had never challenged the likes of Donald before.

During the sign off, Donald had requested to stay on-board for a second contract of four months, whilst the gang of three, exhausted were happy to leave. Donald saw them off the vessel, and waved all three a cheery goodbye. Donald could do a double-header trip. Aggro would never wear him out.

It was during this period that Donald decided that he should be more independent and although he didn't see his parents very often, he thought that he should buy his own property, and certainly nowhere near Bangor. On previous leaves, Donald noticed that his mother and father were becoming institutionalised. Their world appeared to be shrinking, as Ronald was away in Sussex working at a hotel, and his sister Elsie had married the local butcher, and settled into a semi-detached in the posh end of Bangor. Margo especially, had deteriorated both mentally and physically. She had, by far had the better sense of humour, and she never descended into snobbery. Whereas Walter, believed that he must have been swapped at birth, and he really was the illegitimate son of an aristocrat. Margo would love to listen to Donald's sea-going stories which were a little risqué, all the more to have a giggle about. He would sit with Margo in the dining room, whilst father was in the lounge, which he had converted into a treatment room, as he was now a private chiropodist. If Walter walked into the dining room unexpectedly when Donald was in mid flow cheering up his mother. Donald would immediately stop mid-sentence as he knew that Walter's prudish view on life would not gel with any risqué conversations between Donald and his mother. Donald loved his mother, forgiving her, her faults in motherhood. Donald believed that Nanna Fanny was in fact the initial culprit, and father Walter had picked up where Nanna Fanny had left off. Donald was more like his mother in personality, and not like his father at all. Where Ronald followed his father's traits to a T.

Donald could virtually say what he liked to his mother, within reason, and if he considered that stern criticism was meant only to consider her health, both mentally and physically. However, any good that was done, was soon undone when Donald returned to sea.

Donald considered buying a property in Somerset, where Nanna Frieda lived. So he contacted Nanna Frieda and proposed staying with her in her home, whilst he looked for a property to buy in the area.

Nanna Frieda instantly agreed, as she knew that Donald had money, and the rent would come in very handy. A year or two before Grandad Archibald had died, and when Archibald's little Morris Minor car had packed up. Donald bought him another Morris Minor for £50.00. Grandad Archibald, as the true socialist that he was, protested, as he did not want Donald spending money on him. Donald told his Grandad that he would prefer to buy him a little run-around car, instead of wishing that he had done it in twenty years' time, when it would be too late and Grandad would be gone.

Donald had also bought his Nanna and Grandad a new carpet for their lounge, and when Nanna Frieda complained that her suite of furniture had seen better days, Donald told them to put their coats on and they would all three walk to the local furniture shop in Green Bottom and buy a new suite. This is when Grandad Archibald burst into tears, and said that they really did not need a new suite. Donald, seeing how upset that his Grandad was, then suggested that they all go back into the front room. Nanna Frieda was fuming, as she nearly had a new suite from her gullible grandson.

So whilst Donald was living with Nanna Frieda, and Donald was pleased to be generous with paying rent. He did find it eventually financially exhausting as Frieda would be happy with Donald when he gave her money, but became increasingly grasping, and for much shorter and shorter periods between payments, that in the end it would have been cheaper for Donald to have lodged at a four star hotel. However, he endured Nanna Frieda's greed and knuckled down to finding a home of his own.

He eventually found a semi-detached cottage a couple of miles outside of Green Bottom in the village of Pudding Well. It was a two bed cottage on the front road which went through the village. It had a spacious lounge, a dining room, kitchen, two double bedrooms upstairs and a bathroom downstairs.

The back garden was a third of an acre, and the purchase price was £9,950.00.

Donald furnished the cottage with second-hand furniture, a second hand TV, dining room table and chairs, dresser, beds, kitchen cabinet, cooker, and it became a real bachelor pad. For the first time in his life he now had his own place and space.

It was around this time that Donald courted girls that advertised in the dating ads in the newspapers, his leave was short, so time was of the essence.

Donald went out with a girl who sounded really good from her profile, but although she undoubtedly had a lovely disposition, she was not easy on the eye. She wore a blouse, thick buttoned jacket, matching skirt, thick nylon stockings and brown brogues. They went out to a restaurant, and they talked over a meal. Donald noticed her brown eyes, and she informed Donald that she wore contact lenses. Donald unthinkingly then said "Do they also cover the whites of your eyes?" She frowned and said "No, they don't!" They agreed to meet again. However, Donald could not envisage this relationship going any further, even though she was a fantastic pianist and was obviously smitten with Donald.

He went on various other dead-end dates, and thought life at sea was much easier, where you could pick up a girl, and you do not even have to get to know her name, but just enjoy her company for a limited time.

Donald made good friends with an old Somerset couple who lived across the road. They were Mr Stewart Wallace, and Mrs Audrey Wallace, a couple, who were working class. Stewart being a very able and clever engineer (retired) and Audrey a stay at home wife and mother of three grown up children, two girls and a boy.

Stewart was a garrulous man, who wore a flat cap, open necked checked shirt, braces holding up his trousers and walked with a stick, although he was very sprightly. Somerset born and bred. Salt of the earth. He and Donald would go for long walks and discuss politics and life in general. Donald liked the old boy, and he also liked Audrey. As he lived on his own, they would invite Donald over to watch TV with them in their small living room. Stewart would then bring out a bottle of Scotch whisky from the cabinet and both he and Donald would have a small shot each in a glass. All three, would watch the TV, enjoying episodes of Dynasty and Dallas, whilst Stewart would remark how lovely the ladies looked in the soaps. Toward the end of the evening Audrey would get up from her seat, and disappear into her small kitchen, where she had a one ring stove, and a small grill underneath. She would make hot beef sandwiches with mustard, and the smell wafting into the living room would make your mouth water.

She would bring in three plates and together with another glass of whisky, the sandwiches would go down a treat.

Donald bought a second hand Old English White Mark 2 Jaguar, with red leather seats. The car required a complete over-haul, and Donald paid around £2,000 to have the car rebuilt. He also owned a Ford Cortina, using the Jag for special occasions and the Cortina for everyday use. Donald bought these things, not for any snob value, but just because he could afford to. After all he was away at sea for months, sometimes years, and seafarers earned good money in comparison to shore-side workers, and seafarers were better positioned to save money. As whilst they were on-board a vessel, food and board were included in the wages. The salary was also tax free as long as he was out of the country for 6 months out of a year.

Unwittingly, Donald had incurred jealousy from others in the village, although he did not know many people. Nobody likes to think that someone else should have more than them. This Donald found, was usually more apparent in small places rather than big cities, as the small village mentality dictates that everyone knows everybody else's business, gossip and rumour-mongering knowing no bounds.

Stewart and Audrey had three grown up children, Barnaby, the eldest son, then William, and the youngest, a daughter called Sandra. Barnaby was married, and an engineer who worked in Bristol. William was an insurance broker working in Hereford. Sandra lived in Pudding Well around half a mile from her parents. She was a lovely girl, who was married with two sons and a daughter. Sandra used to visit her parents, and as they lived just across the road from Donald, both he and Sandra would see a lot of each other at her parents' house.

She was happily married and was a good girl, and although she and Donald joked together, there was no reason that anyone could suggest any other intimacy when Sandra became pregnant and gave birth to a little girl. There were those who were mean spirited in the village, and openly remarked to Sandra that this new addition to her family looked nothing like her other three children.

CHAPTER SIX
MEDICAL & MISCELLANEOUS

Before Donald had embarked on his medical training course in Liverpool. In order that he gained some medical knowledge so that he would be better prepared. Hospital administrators at a cottage hospital in Bangor, allowed him to work voluntarily on the wards.

Donald wanted lots of varied experience, but he was shown a lot of older patients with leg ulcers. So after a week at the hospital, he became quite an expert on people with leg ulcers. He was not expecting many seafarers to be suffering from that particular condition.

After becoming top of his class at college when gaining his medical certificate. Donald felt prepared for what anyone could throw at him with medical emergencies. His own experience as a patient when he was a Second Cook was a negative moment. When sailing as a Second Cook, he was scrubbing a butcher's block table-top with a wire brush, and one of the rusty prongs gouged into his left hand. He cleaned it up as best he could, and thought nothing more about it. However, the wound became septic, so he went to see the Chief Steward, and the Chief Steward examined the infection, and decided to see if he could burst the abscess that had made the palm of his hand swell. He lanced the wound and used tweezers to probe inside, to see if the poison could be released. The gouged probing for Donald was extremely painful, and over the next few days the pain and swelling worsened. When the vessel docked at Dampier, Western Australia. Port officials boarded the vessel, including a doctor, who was seated in the Captains office. Donald was called to the Captains office to speak to the doctor. The doctor gave a cursory glance, and advised that Donald should attend the clinic in the following morning.

Donald by now was in excruciating pain, but thought, well another twelve hours won't matter. When he was seen by another doctor at the clinic, the physician was aghast that Donald had not been admitted for treatment the night before. In his opinion the infection was serious as he could see a blue line in a vein in the arm which indicated that the infection was well on the move.

Donald underwent antibiotic treatment, and his condition was so severe, that he was admitted into hospital where he stayed for a week. He re-joined the vessel in Singapore. The Master, realising that both he and the Chief Steward had severely under estimated Donald's injury, could not do enough for him on his return.

So now that Donald, himself a Catering Officer and Medical Officer. He wanted to do as well as possible for the crew on the vessel. Donald was popular with both Officers and ratings. He did not hold a grudge with ratings, although his nine years as a rating where a struggle. Donald understood human nature well enough, and realised that there was good and bad in everyone, and that also included the Officers. Some officers were great individuals, whilst others had very poor human traits, although they were better educated than the ratings, it did not mean that they were better people. So Donald was fair to both Officers and ratings, and if he liked someone, it had nothing at all to do with their rank, but more to the disposition and personality of the individual.

Donald was Catering Officer on one of the VLCC tankers that journeyed from Europe to the Middle East and back, and on this ship was a Welsh Chief Engineer called Dai Roberts, who originated from South Wales. He was a family man, with a wife and two children at home.

The Chief Engineer appeared reasonably friendly toward Donald, though Donald kept a weather eye on him, as some Heads of Department tried to undermine the Catering Officer's position.

All was going swimmingly, then one day, there was a leak in one of the pipes in the engine-room, and the best way to detect the leak was to put porridge oats into the system which would swell up and make it easier to detect the area of the leaking pipe that would then require repair.

The Chief Engineer, who wanted to impress his junior engineers in the Officers Bar, shouted to Donald "We want to commandeer your galley and storeroom supply of porridge oats!" The junior engineers soon realised that their Chief was trying to belittle Donald, and were keen to see what Donald would say in response. Donald quiet and with deliberation, calmly informed him that there was no need for any commandeering, all he had to be was be polite and clear with regard to his request. The Chief Engineer blustered, as he then tried to regain control of the situation. He was the Chief Engineer, and therefore an important man on-board the ship. Donald agreed that he was important, but that was no excuse for rudeness. The Chief Engineer, called Donald a Grocer, which was a demeaning insult to the rank of Catering Officer. Donald informed him that the Captain was his line manager, and therefore, if he had a complaint, then he should report it to the Master. Donald had put him in his place. However, Donald did talk to the Master later and reiterated the key points of the confrontation. The Master was in the picture, and trusted Donald sufficiently enough to understand that he was not the protagonist. The Chief Engineer did call at Donald's office, and insisted that he meant no harm. Donald told him, that he believed that he did actually intend to belittle him, but it had not come off as expected. The name of the game, is to stand your ground when your position is threatened, especially if you believe yourself to be in the right.

Needless to say, that the Chief Engineer did not play that same game again.

Donald kept a wary eye on Dai Roberts from then on, and looking at his Bond and bar bill, Donald could not help notice that the Chief Engineer either a raging alcoholic, or was holding wild parties in his cabin every night, and inviting all and sundry to sup his booze.

The ship had orders to call at a port in Saudi Arabia. This Kingdom is strictly Muslim, and their laws regarding the consumption of alcohol are severe. They do allow foreign nationals on-board Merchant ships arriving in Saudi Arabian waters a limited amount of alcohol, which all crew members must declare to customs on a personal effects manifest.

The ship was loading cargo at Jeddah, Saudi Arabia, and initially the loading was going well. Loading time was usually between 24 and 36 hours, so not a long stay in the Kingdom.

However, there was a fuel line fault, and the loading of cargo was halted. This meant that the vessel would stay alongside for another two or three days.

Whilst Donald was sitting at his desk one evening, Chief Engineer Dai Roberts, knocked on his door, and asked if the Bonded Stores was now open. Donald informed him that customs had sealed the Bond, so the sale of any tobacco or alcohol was still prohibited. A frown darkened the Chief Engineer's face, and Donald thought that he saw a flicker of panic in his eyes. The Chief Engineer returned to his own quarters.

Next day, there was the customary weekly fire drill, and whilst Donald was at his lifeboat station, a radio message from the Master came through requesting Donald's presence in the Chief Engineer's cabin. Donald made his way up to the cabin, and upon going through the door, he saw the Captain and Chief Officer were already in attendance and the Chief Engineer was kneeling on the carpet by his desk, chewing the leg! This was a shocking spectacle, and Donald instantly realised that the Chief Engineer was going through delirium tremors, due to a sudden halt of his intake of alcohol.

Embarrassing situation! The Master asked what Donald could do to assist, and Donald recommended sedatives to tide him over.

However, later during the middle of the night toward midnight, the Chief Engineer suffered a relapse, he had telephoned the duty engineer to come to his cabin. The Third Engineer turned up at the Chief Engineer's cabin, and was shocked to see that all of the cabin furniture was in disarray and overturned. The Chief Engineer screamed at him "I have been chasing them, and they have all got away, except one, and he is here in my fridge!" Dai was grimly holding onto the door of the fridge. When the 3rd Engineer asked who he had been chasing? Dai, screamed back "Well, the little green men of course!"

It did not take long for the 3rd Engineer to suspect that the Chief Engineer was craving an alcoholic beverage, so he brought him up a can of beer from his own cabin. The Chief Engineer, swallowed the contents in seconds. It was like feeding an elephant with peanuts. Just not enough!

The Master was advised of the incident, and a helicopter was dispatched from port, landing on the vessel's helicopter deck in the morning and whisking the Chief Engineer and his baggage ashore, so that he could be repatriated to the United Kingdom. The company paid for his eventual stay at a rehabilitation clinic in order to dry him out.

Two years later, whilst Donald was serving on-board a vessel in the North Sea, a new Chief Engineer arrived after Donald had been on the ship for two months, and the Chief Engineer was Dai Roberts.

Donald hoped that he was now a well man, though it was soon apparent that he was up to his old tricks again. Other Officers noticed that he was a habitual drunk, and the cadet officers on-board decided to play a trick on him. The Chief Engineer was fond of Gin, and would swing by the Officers Bar from time to time, put a glass to the gin optic, and take a couple of shots, then drink it neat, and continue out of the bar to his duties. The cadets swapped the gin bottles, half-filling an empty gin bottle with tap water and replacing it in the optic.

The Chief Engineer swung by the bar as usual, picked up a glass, put it to the optic, and downed two shots of pure water. The best bit of it, was that he was totally unaware that it was water he had just drank. Poor devil.

The Captain got wind of the gin scam, he asked Donald, that as he had sailed with Dai Roberts on the very ship that had air-lifted him following his last debacle, why had he not divulged this information to him. Donald replied that as Dai Roberts had been receiving treatment for alcoholism, that it would not have been fair to him, in not giving him a chance to show that he was 'cured' and competent.

This Captain liked Donald, although he did consider that as he had commanded many more vessels that were involved with lightening operations (ship to ship oil transfers involving special experience) and coast operations which was mentally demanding, loading and discharging cargo, and entering and leaving ports in quick succession. The Captain thought that personnel who were in predominantly deep-sea operations had it easy, and they did not require the required cerebral matter that was needed with coastal operations. So he called all deep sea seafarers, 'Deep Sea Baboons'. This Captain wore thick framed black spectacles. So the Chief Officers and other Deck Officers including Donald bought a stack of small stuffed fluffy toys of a monkey for themselves. One day, whilst the deck officers where working on deck, Donald made half a dozen spectacles cut out of from chart paper, and inked the frames black, and then went to each officers' cabins and attached the spectacles to each monkey. All monkeys looked conspicuously like the Captain.

Shortly after, one of the Chief Officers came running to Donald's office with his toy monkey wearing the spectacles. 'Look what somebody has done to my monkey. It looks the spit of the Old Man'. Donald laughed, but little did he know that the Captain had already spotted one of the bespectacled monkeys', though took the slight with a wry smile.

An AB (able bodied seaman) had gashed his hand open, and this was an opportunity for Donald to try out his suturing skills. In a way he was seeking the opportunity as something positive, and never gave much thought that it could be a gruesome task. The AB was taken to the medical locker, and Donald examined the wound. The AB had sustained a deep cut into the palm of his hand. There was no question that the chap required stitches. The AB sat down, clutching a towel around his injured hand, whilst Donald went to arrange the sutures, and equipment in readiness of the operation.

When all was ready, Donald, cleaned the wound, and set about stitching the hand. However, as he was trying to puncture the edges of the wound with the curved needle, the wound gaped and bubbled, and the bones in the hand glistened from within. Donald felt himself becoming hot, in fact very hot and sweaty. He asked the AB if he would like a glass of water, and the AB accepted. Donald went into the smaller medicine room with a sink, he looked into the mirror and saw that his countenance was a nasty grey colour. He slugged back a full glass of cold water, waited a while, and brought back a glass of water for the AB. Donald returned to the task, and fighting back nausea, he completed the task with six sutures.

Donald was on another vessel, where there were British ratings. The Chief Cook was a skinny, angular faced thirty-something, who was not the sharpest tool in the box. As a Petty Officer, the Chief Cook was permitted to bring his wife to sea for a trip. The Chief Cook was called Richard Skillicorn, and his wife's name was Carol. She was around 5ft 5 inches, but she was no Twiggy, she was a rotund lump of a girl.

Richard used to call at Donald's office every morning where they would discuss the following day's menu. Richard was not a man of any imagination, so a lot of the planning was down to Donald. Richard would sit and fidget in a chair by Donald's desk. Donald would look up from his menu book to find Richard busy chewing his finger nails down to the quick. Donald would say "Still hungry, Richard?"

It was not the most hygienic habit for a Chief Cook, but then, this was the guy that Donald had to work with.

The ship called at Abidjan, a port in West Africa. The country was poor. However, the night life was apparently good. The ship was at anchor within port limits, and the crew were allowed shore leave. In order to get ashore, the company had arranged for a launch service from shore to ship and back to shore. A lot of the ratings took the opportunity to go ashore. They had to descend from the vessel by an accommodation ladder, which would take them down to a waiting launch, where they would stretch out between launch and ladder, and then hop aboard. The crew went ashore and on their return at around midnight, they took the launch back to the vessel. The Chief Cook and his wife were in the party of shore-goers, so when they ascended the accommodation ladder to the vessel, Carol, who was wearing heels fell to her knees, on the accommodation ladder. She was wearing black stockings, and she initially thought that her injury was only slight. However, when she was on-board the ship, she felt real pain in her knee. Donald was woken from his sleep by the Chief Cook banging on his door. Richard explained that his wife had injured herself. Donald said that he would meet them at the medical locker.

When Donald cut away the nylon stocking which was encasing Carol's knee, he was shocked to find that the stocking had been holding a large deep cut together. The knee opened up into a bleeding chasm. There was so much fat and flesh, that being soft, had split open like a watermelon. The only obvious answer was that the wound would require stitches.

Carol was laid face up on the hospital operating table, the wound was cleaned, and Donald set about stitching the wound. He then bandaged the leg, and dispensed a course of antibiotics. Donald hospitalised Carol in the ships hospital with its own bathroom facility. He gave firm instructions that she was not to move from the bed on her own, and that her husband would help her with toileting etc. Donald went to see the Captain and reported the incident. The Captain, John Foot, who normally favoured Donald, was angry with him this time, and scolded Donald for suturing Carol's leg, and that Donald, should really have used sellotape, as that would have done the job. Donald did feel aggrieved, as he felt that he had done a good job.

However, as Carol was of similar intellect to her husband Richard, got in and out of her bed for any excuse, and even went to meet the lads in the crew messroom. It was no wonder, that on a visit to the bathroom, that she tripped over the step, and burst open all of her stiches.

This was a good opportunity to consult with the Captain or Head Surgeon. He asked the Captain to come and see Carol, and sought his advice on the best course of action. The Master entered the sick bay, and upon inspection of Carol's gaping wound, was stuck for words. Donald, seeing that the Captain was slow to suggest a remedy, made his own suggestion, asking "Sellotape?" The Master realised that he had been caught by his own hook, and told Donald to carry on and replace the broken stiches with new sutures.

Donald did a second beautiful stitching job, though this time, he strapped two splints to both sides of her leg, so that she could not bend her knee, even if she did fall down again. The wound healed within two to three weeks.

On another occasion, Donald was on-board a vessel that was calling at Batangas in the Philippines. The port security was tight, and there were restrictions on visitors coming into the docks and boarding vessels. Donald had always liked Filipina girls as they were full of fun and very pretty. Donald talked to the on-board Filipino security guard, slipping him a US$10.00 bill into his hand, requesting him to find him one of the local beauties, and brings her back to the ship. The guard went ashore and within the hour he was back. He had brought a gorgeous Filipina girl with him when he came to Donald's office. Donald thanked him, and led the girl into his cabin. They got to know each other, and she accepted a drink. It was not too long before it was time for bed, so Donald suggested an early night. However, whilst snuggling together, the young girl who was in obvious discomfort, and was wincing from time to time. Donald was concerned, and asked what ailed her. She pointed to her mouth and teeth, and it seemed obvious to Donald that she was suffering from toothache. As the pain in her mouth was ruining their evening. Donald asked her to get dressed. They both got dressed, and Donald led the girl to the medical locker, where he sat her down, and asked her to open her mouth wide, while he shone a torch into her mouth to determine the source of the pain. Donald spotted the problem, she had lost a filling, and the cavity was showing infection. Donald set out his kit of dental equipment, and then began cleaning and scraping out the infected cavity. He then mixed a small amount of dental cement, and with some professional sculpting, he completed a very neat temporary filling. She was given pain relief. The recovery was miraculous, she was feeling so much better and without pain. So with a bounce in their step, they left the medical locker together, hand in hand and back to Donald's quarters.

The rest of the evening was pain-free and most enjoyable. Next morning, she was sat happily on Donald's lap with her bowl of cornflakes eating at Donald's desk. The Captain pulled the curtain, peeping in, and then with a wry smile, drew the door curtain and went on his way.

With so many opportunities for seafarers to enjoy the company of beautiful women in many ports of the world. It was not without risk. AIDS was unheard of in the 70's and 80's. But gonorrhoea, syphilis and non-specific urethritis was rife. So there were quite a few occasions when ratings and officers would come to Donald's office with the suspected clap. Donald was on hand with either an injection of penicillin or tetracycline. Of course, there was always a plentiful supply of condoms in the medical locker available for all crew members. Though for some, the fiddling with condoms was too much bother for some of the seafarers, so they gambled, and sometimes compromised their sexual health.

Donald had to admit that he himself had been at fault on one occasion, and had been at the serious end of a penicillin needle.

CHAPTER SEVEN
POLITICAL VIEWPOINT

When Donald was a teenager he had come across a notable text that had been written during the middle ages, a timeless code of advice on the best way to tackle life, and to survive the ordeal, and come through the experience reasonably intact. Simple guidelines, but not so simple due to human frailties, and this includes Donald's own fragility and imperfections. Nevertheless, timeless words that rang true in the sixteenth century, that ring true today and will ring true in tomorrow's world. Here follows the words from Desiderata:

GO PLACIDLY amid the noise and haste, and remember what peace there may be in silence. As far as possible, without surrender, be on good terms with all persons.
Speak your truth quietly and clearly; and listen to others, even to the dull and the ignorant; they too have their story.

Avoid loud and aggressive persons; they are a vexatious to the spirit. If you compare yourself with others, you may become vain or bitter, for always there will be greater and lesser persons than yourself.

Enjoy your achievements as well as your plans. Keep interested in your own career, however humble; it is a real possession in the changing fortunes of time.

Exercise caution in your business affairs, for the world is full of trickery. But let this not blind you to what virtue there is; many persons strive for high ideals, and everywhere life if full of heroism.

Be yourself. Especially do not feign affection. Neither be cynical about love; for in the face of all aridity and disenchantment, it is as perennial as the grass.

Take kindly the counsel of the years, gracefully surrendering the things of youth.

Nurture strength of spirit to shield you in sudden misfortune. But do not distress yourself with dark imaginings. Many fears are born of fatigue and loneliness.

Beyond a wholesome discipline, be gentle with yourself. You are a child of the universe no less than the trees and the stars; you have a right to be here.

And whether or not it is clear to you, no doubt the universe is unfolding as it should. Therefore be at peace with God, whatever you conceive Him to be. And whatever yours labours and aspirations, in the noisy confusion of life, keep peace in your soul. With all its sham, drudgery and broken dreams, it is still a beautiful word. Be cheerful. Strive to be happy.

From a very early age, Donald had always been interested in politics. Maybe it was due to the fact that Grandad Archibald had been a fervent politician. He had been the Labour Party agent for the West Somerset Member of Parliament. Archibald had also been a District Councillor, and a Chairman of the Magistrates bench. Archibald had been a lifetime and fervent socialist. This was during the time when socialism was a definite requirement for western democracies. When there was a big divide between the haves and the have nots, and Archibald had been a true crusader, fighting against any injustice that was meted out to people who could not defend themselves. He was adored by the ordinary people of West Somerset, because they saw him as a fighter against poverty, against oppression and bringing justice and fairness for the many, and not just the few. The words sound familiar in today's Labour Party, but unfortunately in this modern era, the Labour movement only rattle out the old slogans, as the slogans are no longer as relevant as they were in the 1920's and the 1930's. The world has changed, and the Labour Party have lost their way, wanting to achieve a Marxist regime, which proved to be a social failure in the Soviet Union and in China. They have let the electorate down in not being a relevant opposition party, who should be challenging the Conservative Government more effectively, by understanding that the British people on the whole, are of moderate politics, and want neither a Communist leadership nor a Fascist Dictatorship. A great shame that the Labour Party have become entrenched into idealistic left wing ideals do not match with the principles of the electorate. From Donald's point of view, political parties should encourage people to independence and personal freedom, and never allow any politician or government to control their lives for a political dogma. However, in Grandad Archibald case, when the world was a different place, he practiced what he preached. There were no double standards. He had no desire to become rich with cash, but he was definitely rich in humanity. He would give his last penny to help out another person, and he sought nothing in return. That is true socialism!

Donald had come across many pseudo socialists in his time, who espoused socialism on one hand, though were the meanest of people, who took and grabbed as much as they could lay their hands on, and gave nothing back at all. They then had the impertinence to say that Tory supporters and Tory politicians were scum, and were the people, who robbed the poor. True to a point, years ago, but nothing like it in today's world.

Donald remembered his next door neighbour in Pudding Well, who was a fervent labour supporter. He worked for the local council as a road maintenance driver. The neighbour noticed that Donald had left his wheelbarrow in the garden for a few days, and thinking that the wheelbarrow was redundant, asked if he could have it. Douglas informed him that he still required the use of the wheelbarrow.

The neighbour at another time, who owned a much smaller garden than Donald, asked if he could purchase half of Donald's own garden, though he never made an actual offer of cash. Donald declined to sell, though he did advise the neighbour that he would allow the him to move the adjoining fence outward from the his side of the property by 3ft width and 60ft length into Donald's own garden, and Donald offered this land area 'free of charge'. The neighbour could not believe his good fortune, and within a week he had moved the boundary. The morale of this particular story is that although the left wing of the Labour Party degrade Tories as scum. Tories are by and large, good people, who in reality practice and carry out socialism in a very positive manner. You don't have to be a supporter of the Labour Party to be a socialist. Socialism belongs to everybody. The difference is that the Conservative Party will help anyone, but people also have to help themselves. The world owes no one a living, and we all have a certain responsibility to put into the community without always considering what can be taken out from it.

Donald had been a member of the Conservative Party for many years, and was a great admirer of Mrs Margaret Thatcher. He would watch the TV, and listen to the speeches when Mrs Thatcher was leader of the opposition, during the Labour Government lead by sunny Jim Callaghan, who Donald also respected. So when it was time for the General Election, and an opportunity for the election of a Conservative government. Donald at that time was home on leave, and took the opportunity in becoming involved with canvassing votes for the local Conservative Party in West Somerset. The Conservative candidate for West Somerset, was Peter Cartland. Donald offered the Conservative Group his home, to be used as a committee room for the duration of the campaign. Donald met the Tory candidate, Peter Cartland, a wealthy Somerset gentleman farmer. He also met Peter's younger sister, called Blossom. She was a vivacious girl with lots of energy, and keen to help her brother win the election for West Somerset. Donald canvassed with Blossom, and the two became good friends. It was a fiercely fought election, but well worth the fight, as Mrs Thatcher and the Conservative Party won the vote by a huge landslide.

However, three years following the election. Donald had his own business, and the government had increased the business rates, and there were other challenges that affected small business at that particular time. Also the village of Pudding Well, being built in a valley and surrounded by forestry on all sides, suffered from very poor and erratic TV reception. From Donald's point of view, if the government was going to increase local rates, then the people should have better services. It was, in Donald's opinion, that there should be a balance, if something is a negative, then balance it with a positive. So Donald wrote a letter to the MP that he had helped to win the seat representing West Somerset.

Peter Cartland wrote back and said that he would be happy to meet to discuss the situation. A date was set for Peter to come to Donald's house for a meeting. However in the interim, Donald had formulated a group of other villagers who felt the same way about the lack of TV reception and the need of a TV mast to be erected on the ridge of the village which would enhance the TV signal for the people of the village and beyond. The newly formed committee, called themselves 'The Pudding Well Action Group'.

Peter Cartland duly arrived at Donald's house where he was warmly welcomed. Afternoon tea had been laid on for him, and there were lots of smiles and bonhomie. The group put their position to the MP, who listened patiently, though was not forthcoming with any promise of furthering the Action Group's cause. In fact on the way out of the house, Peter told Donald that no one would be interested in this particular grievance, and really he was not too bothered that anything should be done at all. Donald thanked him for his visit and saw him to his Range Rover.

Peter's words were a disappointment, which gave Donald an idea, that he should write about the meeting and send the information to the local newspaper. Donald wrote to the Green Bottom Chronicle and made a point in saying that their MP had treated the action group, like 'Peasants and Imbeciles'. He then posted the letter to the newspaper editor.

A few days passed and Donald had quite forgotten about the letter. Upon returning home one afternoon, he received a phone call, and the voice of Peter Cartland boomed out angrily, saying "What do you mean? That I treated you all like peasants and imbeciles?" "Oh" Donald said "so, they published my letter then?" "Well Mr Cartland, you told me, when you were at my house, that nobody would be interested in our protest, well it seems that the newspapers are interested" "After all Mr Cartland, I canvassed for you during the last election, and in fact I know your sister Blossom, very well!" "You don't remember me, do you?" "But you'll remember me know, won't you?" Peter Cartland spluttered back angrily "But, but…." Donald cut him off saying "Well Mr Cartland, I understand politics well enough, and I have only done to you, what you would have done to me, but I got in there first!" With that, Peter Cartland slammed down the phone.

Following the telephone, the national papers took up the story, and photographers arrived at Donald's home, and the family where treated to a photoshoot which made national news.

Within a period of two months, a TV mast had been erected on the ridge of the village, and everyone in the village and beyond were treated to brilliant TV reception, no more snowy and grainy images. Perfect crisp colour. As the saying goes. 'The pen is mightier than the sword.' Well it certainly was in this case.

Donald never liked political correctness. His interpretation on the imposition of PC, was that democratic countries were struggling and juggling with the rights of free speech. Concerned that people, having their own opinion, may upset the status quo. For countries that were controlled by one party states, their populace did not need to practice political correctness, as in fact they did not dare to open their mouths at all and criticise the state, or anything else that was not in the party manifesto. So western democracies have used PC as a tool to supress free speech, and it has been incredibly effective as many people are followers rather than thinkers, and do not question orders. So when democracies appear free and just, it is basically a very thin veneer of respectability. There are double standards, and hypocrisy is considered the norm. Donald does not suggest or recommend revolt, but he would certainly recommend that everyone can and should state their case honestly and sincerely. Not to skirt around contentious issues, so that debates just go around and around in circles, and the participants, whilst considering political correctness, water down their beliefs and arguments. The truth then does not come across, and nothing at all is resolved. This is the reason why populist politicians thrive in today's world. Democracies only take an avid interest in the electorate when campaigning for election into government. When an election has passed, they forget their promises and obligations to the electorate, and just career build for themselves. People have tired of this type of politics, and look for people who speak their language, who understand their frustrations and concerns, and who speak openly and honestly, and are not constrained by Political Correctness.

Nobody wants hate speeches, and vulgar rants that are meant to upset people. But people do want to be able to practice their rights, freedom of speech without fear of condemnation and humiliation.

CHAPTER EIGHT
LIFE ASHORE

Shell Tankers as with a lot of British Shipping Companies during this period where going through a transition. British Officers and ratings were becoming an expensive commodity. So shipping companies began to look for cheaper labour which meant the demise of the British seafarer, and more opportunities of employment for seafarers from the Philippines, Eastern Europe and Hong Kong.

The rank of Chief Steward/Catering Officer was slowly being replaced with the rank of Cook Steward, which meant that the Chief Cooks could be promoted to Cook Steward, and Chief Stewards and Catering Officers would be demoted accordingly. The rank of Radio Officer was also being replaced and renamed as an Electrical Engineer, as there was no requirement for Morse code, now that telecommunications had improved greatly with on-board fax machines, GPS etc.

So it was with regret that Donald considered voluntary redundancy, as he was not filled with enthusiasm to grasp the role of Cook Steward. He had worked so hard for Officer Status. In hindsight, he should have given it more thought, as the new role would have really been a positive move in the long term.

So he resigned when on-board a vessel, and was airlifted by helicopter within port limits off Cape Town, South Africa, and he was repatriated home.

With the redundancy money of £11,000.00 which was a lot of money in those days. Donald paid to have an extension built onto his home, which included a third bedroom, a large patio and a garage (with an inspection pit), and small office.

One of the young builders named Jeff, who was around 18 years old, introduced Donald to his single mother, a lady 5 years older than Donald, called Barbara. She was a very smart lady, who dressed well, around 5ft 5 inches tall, a brunette, and always wore make up, which was beautifully applied. It was not long before Barbara moved in with Donald, and Jeff her son, had his own room. All three were a ready-made family. Before long, Donald asked Barbara for her hand in marriage, buying a £500 sapphire and diamonds engagement ring, and she agreed. A wedding date was set, with a honeymoon arranged for a week in Cyprus. Though, in the run-up to the anticipated wedding, on the various walks that Donald, Barbara and Jeff would take. Jeff would pipe up to Donald when he spotted someone he knew, saying "Mum has been with him!" No problem for Donald, as he himself had been around the block a few times himself. However, when Jeff repeated the same statement on many other occasions whenever they would bump into the many beaus that his mother had cohabitated with, the relationship between Donald and Barbara, seemed to unravel like a badly knitted cardigan. The final insult was when Donald found out that Barbara had been shacking up with other guys during the week. So of course the wedding was off the cards. Donald let Barbara keep the engagement ring. She made good use of the honeymoon booking in Cyprus and went there on a holiday, enjoying a fling while on the honeymoon isle with a Libyan guy.

When one door closes, another one opens. This happened around two months after Barbara and Donald parted company. Donald was out and about in Taunton, and was in one of the local pubs in the town, and as it was a Saturday night, there was a karaoke taking place on the raised stage in the lounge bar. Donald limited himself to lemonade shandy as he was driving. Various people had already been on the stage and their singing left a lot to be desired, as many of them were out of tune. Then a blond girl took the stage, with another girl who was short and dumpy. They started to sing 'Dancing Queen' the Abba song. Whilst the short dumpy girl had no musical tone whatsoever, the tall blond girl sang like an angel. Donald was immediately struck with this girl, there was something that was vulnerable about her which Donald found attractive. He waited until the song had ended, and the girls left the stage and went back to their seats. Donald left it a few minutes, and then went to the bar to order another drink. He went by the table that the girls were sitting, and up to the blond girl, asking if he could treat both ladies to a drink. The blond girl looked up, startled..... "Well, yes, OK" she stammered. She asked for a dry martini and lemonade, with more lemonade that martini. The short stumpy girl asked if she could have a pint of bitter. Donald went to the bar and ordered the drinks, and brought them back to their table. He asked if he could join them, and they both acquiesced.

Donald introduced himself, and the blond girl said that her name was Penelope, and that her friend's name was Lorraine. They both lived in a village called Milverton which was around 7 miles outside of Taunton.
There was a lot of small talk at the table, as it was difficult for any in-depth conversation, two lads had just got on the stage, obviously well oiled, singing and shouting out that they would 'never walk alone'.
Penelope seemed initially charmed with Donald, as he could pull out all the stops in charm when he put his mind to it. She laughed when Donald had noticed that Penelope was wearing a green earing in one ear and a red one in the other. He asked if that was the trend in non-matching earrings. Penelope reddened, and Donald regretted bringing the mismatch to her attention, as he did not want to make her feel awkward. Penelope felt the earrings with her hand, and laughed out loud. She said that she had been in a rush to catch the bus, and hadn't noticed that she had put earrings on from two separate pairs.
She explained that she had lost her husband the year before, and had two young children that she was raising now as a single mother. A daughter of 5 called Belinda and a boy of 2 ½ years called Archie.
Donald felt sympathy for her in that he husband had died so young due to heart problems.
They chatted for another 30 minutes, and Donald expressed an interest in meeting with Penelope again, so she gave Donald her phone number to contact her. Donald got up from the table and bid the girls goodnight, and said how delighted that he had been to meet them both.

Donald left the pub with a spring in his step. He was really interested in seeing more of Penelope.

As he was still out of work, he looked at all the job ads in the local newspapers, and attended a few interviews. The jobs that he applied for where not really that interesting and would not be a challenge.

He used to drive to and from an interview in his white jaguar, and prospective employers just said that they would be in touch, but nothing came of the jobs.

In the village of Lyng, a mile from Donald's home in Pudding Well, Donald noticed a disused shed, with a corrugated tin roof which stood on the main road in the middle of the village. The locals said that it used to be a Fish & Chip shop, run by two old ladies, who cooked the best fish & chips for miles around from a coal fired pan fryer. It had been in disrepair for many years and was just a dilapidated shack. Donald investigated who now owned the shed, and set about considering purchasing it with a view of turning it back into a Fish & Chip shop.

He located the owner of the shed, and telephoned him to express his interest on purchasing the shed and land if the property was for sale. The owner said that the shed was indeed for sale, and offered Donald the property for £10,000. Donald was shocked at this price, as this was the sum that he had paid for his newly modernised home a few years before. He pointed out to the owner that the price was exorbitant and ended the call.

In the meantime, Donald looked again for employment, but nothing was available. Around a month after his last query to the owner of the shed, he telephoned him again, and explained that £10,000 was too much, but if he agreed to a sale price of £6,000 for the Freehold, then Donald would buy the property. The owner agreed. Donald then procured legal assistance with the sale, and in the end reduced the sale price down to £5,500.

Once the sale had been concluded. Donald then created a business plan for a bank loan, sufficient to rebuild the shed and convert it into a modern fish & chip takeaway. The bank agreed a loan of £25,000, and Donald then started looking for equipment to kit the shop. A new two pan cooking range would cost £10,000 and was beyond Donald's budget, so he looked through the Exchange &

Mart, and a two pan cooking range from a fish & chip shop in Bolton was for sale, as the shop was closing down. The price was £1,000. Donald, hired builders, who had worked for him in the past, and they travelled from Somerset to Bolton by Ford Transit to purchase the range. The range had been dismantled, ready for transportation. The unit was taken to Donald's home and stored in his garage. During the days that followed, Donald cleaned the range until it shone. He then placed the aluminium chimney vets onto the green outside his home, and stuffing newspapers into the chimney, he set fire to it. The fire caught quickly and the chimney belched flames and black smoke. The heat was melting the animal fat that was the preferred choice in the north of England for frying fish & chips, whereas in the south, palm oil was the preferred option.

Whilst the Fish & Chip Shop was being refurbished, and amid the long wait for planning permission and all the legal necessities involved. Donald pursued his courtship with Penelope. He was invited to her house for dinners, and met Penelope's children, and Donald took time for the children to become used to him. He would read them stories when it was time for their bed, and found that he enjoyed this totally new experience of associating with children, and thought more about settling down with a family one day. Donald and Penelope were becoming closer as time went on, and they became extremely fond of each other, and eventually fell in love. As Penelope had her own house, just a few miles from Donald's home, it was easy for them to see each other on many occasions. Penelope coming over to Donald's home, or Donald stopping over with Penelope and the children.

Donald met Penelope's parents Danny and Gwen. A lovely couple who instantly liked Donald, and made him very welcome at their home. They lived in the same village as Penelope, and had rented the same semi-detached council house from new, which was of a prefabricated construction built in 1948 as the country was still in financial arrears following the end of the Second World War.

CHAPTER NINE
CHAUFFEUR EXTRAORDINAIRE

Still looking for temporary work whilst the shop was under-going renovation. Donald spotted an advert in the local newspaper. A gentleman was looking for a chauffeur to drive him to and from work every day from Taunton to Frome. Donald applied by telephoning the number advertised and spoke to his prospective new employer, a man called Douglas Plodd. Mr Plodd asked Donald to meet him at the Queen Anne Pub in Taunton town centre at 7pm that evening. Donald went to the pub and arrived ten minutes early, and awaited the arrival of Douglas Plodd. Douglas arrived, and they met at the bar. Donald offered Douglas a drink, and he accepted. They found a table and sat together for an informal chat. Douglas was an easy man to talk to. A well-dressed man in his fifties, who was articulate and it was apparent to Donald that this was an educated man with good schooling. He later learned that Douglas had been a pupil at the same school as Prince Charles, Gordonstoun School in Moray, Scotland.

Donald explained his situation in that as he was looking for a temporary position, this also suited Douglas, who only required a chauffeur for a limited time, as he was a drink drive case, and needed a driver whilst he served his driving ban.

Douglas offered Donald the positon, who accepted it gratefully. He was to drive a dark blue, automatic Daimler saloon with white leather seats. The car certainly looked posh enough, though there was an engine issue, in that oil would leak from the engine at an alarming rate. So in order to counteract this defect, Donald had to ensure that around 5 litres of oil was stored in the boot, and available to top up the engine as and when required.

Douglas was a financial director and partner in a firm that specialised in liquid rubber. The firm was called UNIFLEX, and the product had been invented by Douglas' business partner, Jack Russell. In order to give as much publicity to this new invention, Douglas appeared on the 'Tomorrows World' programme and the product was given an upbeat advertising slot. The rubber could be used to seal roofs, guttering, swimming pools, fish ponds etc. The administrative offices were in Frome, near Bath, and it was Donald's job to drive Douglas to and from work every week day. He would also be given a position as 'Customer Services Manager' at UNIFLEX, which involved taking calls from the general public and dealing with any complaints about the product. Donald also had to make samples by pouring the liquid rubber onto silicone paper, and cutting up the cured sheets of rubber, ready for distribution to prospective clients.

When Donald was taking calls from the general public about the product. He received a call from one angry customer who informed Donald that when he had painted the product on his very large fish pond, and then purchased thousands of pounds worth of Koi Carp for the pond. He was distraught, when he woke up one morning, and went to admire his pond and Koi Carp. To find that all the fish were dead, and floating on the surface. It appeared that the product had emitted noxious toxins during the curing process. Needless to say, that UNIFLEX deleted the text from its sales leaflet where it had previously claimed that it was fine for ponds.

Donald was not only employed by Douglas as a chauffeur and customer service manager, but he also acted as a valet. Douglas had complained that his electric razor was malfunctioning, and so when Donald met him at his home to drive him to the office. Douglas handed Donald the razor with the instruction that when they arrived at Frome, Donald must take it to the shop, where it was purchased and arrange for it to be repaired. To explain before going any further. Douglas was an academic, and like a lot of very clever people, he did lack practical skills, and basic common sense. When Donald took the electric razor into the shop for repair. He noticed that it was a high end establishment, and he walked up to a spotless glass counter, and behind the counter stood a smartly dressed, dapper middle-aged man in a three-piece suit. Donald explained to the salesman that his boss had asked him to bring the razor in for repair. The man took the razor from Donald, and held it a second or two, looking quizzically at it, he then unscrewed the lid from the main body, and as soon as the two separated, a deluge of Douglas' beard clippings descended all over the spotless glass counter. The salesman looked up and said to Donald "Maybe you should ask your boss to clean out the razor from time to time!" Donald apologised, picking up the razor and silently withdrew from the shop feeling a little somewhat embarrassed.

In order to publicise the product effectively, Donald was assigned with the Marketing Director, Paul Taylor to visit the home of a photographer of a prominent DIY magazine, who had offered to take publicity photographs involving the application of the liquid rubber onto his garage roof. The photography session would be free, and in exchange, the coating of UNIFLEX on the roof would be free of charge to the photographer. Both Paul and Donald were dressed in work clothes. Checked shirts, jeans and safety shoes. They both looked the part dressed manual labourers (who were supposed to know what they were doing). On arrival at a spacious detached residence, Paul and Donald where met by the photographer and his lovely wife. They were given a cup of tea, before then starting on the project. Both climbed up a ladder onto the flat garage roof. There were old chippings that needed removing before the liquid rubber could be applied. The task looked indeed long and laborious, and Donald in particular estimated that it would take around two hours to bag up the chippings and take the bags, one by one, down the ladder for eventual disposal. Donald said to Paul "Look Paul, there is scrubland just down there over the boundary fence. How about that we just shovel the chippings down there from the roof?" Paul was shocked, as he was not a manual worker, but a business executive, who was better suited behind a desk. However, with a nod, he agreed. Donald started shovelling the chippings off the roof and into the scrubland. Paul looked on for a few seconds, and then with his own shovel, the two of them feverishly scraped up all the chippings, tipping them over the fence, before anyone would notice. They laughed together in the car on the return journey about the experience. Though during the application of the liquid rubber, Donald was the model for the photoshoot. No requirement for any real posing and posturing, as the photos only showed a checked shirt cuff, a gloved hand, holding a brush applying rubber to a roof!

The photographer and his wife treated Paul and Donald to a sumptuous buffet lunch in thanks for their brilliant endeavours.

During a wintry and freezing January, Douglas had allowed Donald to keep the Daimler at his own home for the weekend, so Donald was driving to Douglas' house in the Daimler to pick him up for the usual journey to the office in Frome. That morning the weather was bitterly cold, and there was a threat of ice on the roads. As Donald drove the Daimler around the windy lanes, all was going well until the Daimler's tyres hit a patch of black ice. The effect was immediate, the Daimler spun around and left the road on its own volition, and leapt across a ditch, landing heavily through a hedge into the adjoining field. Donald was shaken. In those days there were no mobile phones, so Donald staggered out of the car and made his way to the nearest house. Knocking on the door, he explained the situation to the owners, and asked if he could use their telephone. Donald telephoned Douglas, and told him of the accident. A tow truck company was asked to attend and the Daimler was towed to their garage for repair. Douglas and Donald then hired a car for their onward journey to Frome.

On one occasion when Douglas was sitting in the back of the limousine (He always opted for the back seat, and never sat next to Donald.) Donald had stopped at a garage to fill the car with petrol. While they waited in a queue, Douglas noticed a young mechanic working under the bonnet of a vehicle. He said to Donald "You know Donald, I have often thought that I would like to be practical with my hands like that young chap." Douglas then mulled over his own musing for a second or two, then added "Hmm, well maybe not!" There was a little bit of the snob value with Douglas, who liked the finer things in life, and really would never consider swapping a life of privilege for a dirty manual job. Douglas never failed to amuse Donald with his little quips.

As Douglas had chosen Donald, because it suited him, Douglas was not aware that Donald had no sense of direction. There was no natural compass element within Donald. He could get lost in a one bedroomed apartment! So when Douglas asked Donald to drive him to an obscure town somewhere in Devon, the journey became more of a mystery tour rather than a simple case of travel from A to B.

They set off from Frome one late afternoon on a rain filled day, and the rain teemed down throughout the journey. Douglas slept in his usual positon at the back, and after an hour or so, he woke, and asked Donald if we had arrived. Donald, who had been unsure along that he had been travelling in the right direction, and not wanting to upset his boss unduly. Spotting a sign pointing to the town centre. Donald said "Nearly there! Just approaching the town centre." Donald sank back in his seat with relief. However, there was only one tiny issue that came to the forefront. It wasn't the town centre they wanted. They were totally off the beaten track and in the wrong town. Donald had to wait another hour whilst Donald struggled to re-calculate his mental compass settings.

When Douglas was in a stroppy mood, he could easily become truculent, and took his moods out on Donald. During long journey's Douglas would pipe up and say to Donald "Do you like the look of the back of that lorry in front?" Donald would realise that Douglas was fed up with the journey, so within seconds, he would veer the Daimler out from the lorry to overtake the vehicle, while Douglas, who was now wide awake, squealing, "Look out! There's a car coming the other way!" Overtaking was a successful operation, though a little bit hairy. Douglas attempted another sarcastic comment, when he asked Donald on another journey, whether he liked nature. Donald was puzzled with the question, and asked his boss why the question. Douglas responded, "Well, you keep taking me into the hedgerows!" He considered that Donald drove far too close to the verge.

Douglas was not bad looking, but certainly no movie star, though he was bit of a ladies man. Even though he had a girlfriend at home, he did like the company of other women. Part of Donald's job was to take Douglas to various places so that Douglas could wine and dine. There was a restaurant called 'The Beaujolais' in the centre of Frome, and Douglas had made arrangements to meet with a young lady for lunch at the restaurant. The town had a one way system, and there were no parking near to the restaurant. Douglas' suggestion was for Donald to navigate the one way system in an hour's time, and slowly drive past the restaurant. Should Douglas not be quite ready, and lunch still on-going, he would signal to Donald from the restaurant window, for him to go around the town's one way system again. Donald waited for an hour as he had found a parking spot on the other side of town. Looking at his watch, he decided that as an hour had passed, he would set off for the restaurant. Approaching slowly as instructed, he saw Donald and the young lady sitting at a table near the window. Donald tooted the horn, Douglas looked round, and then with an elegant wave of his hand, he indicated that Donald go around the one way system again. Donald performed this performance twice again, with the same response, and on the fourth rendezvous, and feeling truly pissed off, it was with relief that Douglas and the young lady were waiting for him on the pavement outside the restaurant.

On another occasion when Douglas wanted to spend time eating on his own in a restaurant for evening dinner. Donald would wait in the Daimler listening to the radio. The time passed, and after around one and a half hours, Donald noticed the pub door opening, and a man walking across the car park towards the Daimler. Donald rolled down the driver's window, and the man, who turned out to be the restaurant manager said "Please can you come in and collect your boss?" Donald followed him back into the pub and through to the restaurant. There he found Douglas, collapsed under a table where a lady and gentleman were sat together. Looked like Douglas had been making a pest of himself. The restaurant manager help Donald hoist Douglas to his feet, and Donald hauled his boss across the car park and tossed him into the back seat of the Daimler.

On another occasion, Douglas had to attend a funeral of a friend who had recently passed away. They had to make an early start, as the funeral was taking place at Milton Keynes. They set off as planned, though Douglas was not in his funeral attire, and was dressed in casual clothing, thinking that as there was plenty of time, he would change at a restaurant bathroom on the way to the funeral. The traffic was incredibly busy that day, and the going was slow. They stopped quickly for a quick take-away burger at McDonalds and carried on. However, the deadline for the funeral was approaching fast, and as the Daimler was winding its way through the streets of Milton Keynes, they found themselves behind the hearse that was taking Douglas' friend to the church. Douglas sat up and shouted to Donald "For God's sake overtake that hearse! I've got to get there before Oscar (his deceased friend) arrives!" Donald put his foot down and accelerated past the hearse at great speed, whilst Donald was struggling to change into his suit trousers at the back of the car. They arrived at the crematorium around three minutes ahead of Oscar.

On another occasion, Douglas wanted to travel to the Carlton Club in London. This was an exclusive gentleman's club in central London. Douglas was attending a function and the guest speaker was the cabinet minister, Norman Tebbit who would be giving a talk on how to find employment, especially if you were the owner of a push bike. The plan was that Donald would spend the night at the Club, whilst Donald would book a room at the Merchant Navy Hotel in Earls Court. Donald as an ex Merchant Seafarer was a life member of the hotel, and could make use of the accommodation and its facilities.

Donald dispatched Douglas at his club, then drove the Daimler to the Merchant Navy Hotel for the night. As mentioned earlier, the Daimler had an engine leak, in that the motor required topping up with engine oil on a regular basis, otherwise the engine would seize up.

The next afternoon, Donald drove from the Merchant Navy Hotel to the Carlton Club to pick up Douglas. They met as scheduled, and then made their way back to Somerset to Douglas' home. On the way up the M4 and then onto the M5, all was going well, and Douglas was asleep in the back of the car. The day was coming to an end and it was getting dark, when they were nearing Taunton. Suddenly, whilst driving in the fast lane, there was a loud clang, and a nasty growling coming from the engine. The oil light was flashing blue, and Donald made rapid lane changes from the fast lane, middle lane then to the slow lane, and eventually stopping on the hard shoulder. Douglas was still sleeping peacefully, whilst Donald got out of the car, opened the bonnet and a flash of flame emerged, setting the engine on fire. Donald wrenched the rear door open, and shouted at Douglas to get out. Douglas groggily came round, and allowed Donald to man handle him out of the car. "Give me your coat!" said Donald to Douglas, whilst ripping the heavy overcoat from Douglas' back, and putting the coat over the engine, and smothering the flames. The fire went out, but the car was not going anywhere. Donald told Douglas, who was still a little hung over from his lunchtime session at the Carlton Club, stood groggily by the car. Donald walked up to the highway phone to call the motorway police for a tow truck. Douglas shouted at Donald "Tell them to put you through to Lord Battersby, he's a friend of mine, and will come to help!" Whilst Donald struggled to talk to the Police, Douglas still harped on that he wanted to speak to Lord Battersby. Donald advised the police officer on the line that his boss insisted on talking to his aristocratic friend. But the policeman informed him that the motorway phone was not a forwarding call service. A tow truck had been requested, and they awaited its arrival. Douglas returned to the back seat and Donald to the driver's seat. Eventually a tow truck turned up, and parked in front of the Daimler. Donald rolled down the front passenger window to talk to the tow truck driver. The driver leaned into the window to talk.

Douglas took immediate affront and said to the tow-driver "Get your hands off my car!" Both Donald and the truck driver taken aback by this unreasonable outburst. The driver backed off, and Donald got out of the car to apologise for his bosses rudeness. The driver was not pleased at all with the confrontation, but said to Donald "Right, get your boss to sit in the back of my cab, and you can sit with me in the passenger seat next to me." Donald returned to the Daimler, and passed on the request to Douglas that he should sit in the tow truck. Douglas was not having any of it, and said that the man could haul the Daimler onto the flat-board behind the cabin of the truck, and he would stay inside the Daimler throughout the journey back. The Driver heard the remark, and said to Donald "Tell him to get his arse into the truck, otherwise I am off and leaving him and his car here!" Donald could see that the driver was at his wits end, and there was really probable that they would both be left stranded on the hard shoulder for the rest of the night. Douglas acquiesced, and he sat behind the driver and Donald sat on the bench seat at the front of the cab. The Daimler was hauled onto the flat-bed and then anchored down safely. The trio set off for the remainder of the journey. Donald made small talk with the driver out of politeness. Douglas heard the interaction and shouted from the back "Don't speak to him Donald!"

The rest of the journey carried on in absolute silence.

Douglas and his business partner Jack wanted to sell the business. This was good news for Douglas. Although his fortunes had soared and waned throughout his working life, he could do with extra funds. Both partners could split the proceeds from the sale of the company, and net them both a few million pounds each.

They eventually found a buyer. Sterling Roncraft, bought out UNIFLEX. It was time now for both partners to celebrate the success of the sale, and they arranged to meet representatives of the buyers at a restaurant in Cardiff for a celebration lunch.

Donald drove both Jack and Douglas down to Cardiff, and to the restaurant. They went in for their lunch, whilst Donald waited in the car for their eventual return.

The lunch lasted for around four hours, and then Jack and Douglas returned to the car. Jack appeared none the worse for drink, though Douglas was flushed and looked like he was three sheets to the wind.

They settled into the back of the limousine, and Donald set off for the return drive to Somerset. Douglas was garrulous, chatting away drunkenly to Jack. Then Douglas piped up to Donald, saying "Don't you wish that you were as successful as us?" Donald gave this question some thought, then replied "No, not really, you're not a good advertisement on how to conduct yourself in public!" With that, Douglas said no more, and slumped back into his seat for a sleep. During the drive back, Donald would look in the mirror and see Douglas' head lolling from side to side. So every time that there was a right hand turn, Douglas' face would slap against the window. Jack noticing these events, and said to Donald "I see that you are helping Douglas kiss the window!" Jack was amused, and so was Donald.

Six months working for Douglas had been an interesting experience for Donald. Notwithstanding Douglas' little foibles, he was a tremendous character, and Donald had grown to like him over this period of employment as chauffeur. Even though the mental anguish that Douglas caused Donald on occasion inclined him to stop at the Green lights and to go at the Stop lights!

CHAPTER TEN
DONALD'S PLAICE

Following Donald's departure as chauffeur. The shed that he had purchased the previous year was now nearing completion of a complete refurbishment. He saw more of Penny and the children, as during this period, they had all moved in with Donald. It seemed the right time, and although at the beginning of the arrangement, Donald had acted more like a bachelor. He had never been used to 'family life' as such. Penelope would have to remind Donald that he was responsible also for little Archie and Belinda. Belinda was an intelligent five year old girl. An old head on young shoulders. She was perceptive and never missed anything. A good listener, pretty and blond, and a real achiever. She always put her heart and soul into everything that she did. It was easy for Donald to become very fond of her. Archie on the other hand was a cheeky blond little boy, who loved playing with his toy cars and busied himself with whatever he was doing without distraction. It was sad that they had lost their father. Belinda had taken the loss badly, as she had been old enough to feel the loss, so she missed her dad very much. However, Donald endeavoured to learn how to become a substitute father figure as quickly as possible, as he knew that Penny fretted for the children, and wanted them to have as near perfect an upbringing as possible, and to be as happy as they could be.

They settled into domestic bliss, and even had a little Jack Russell terrier called Lady. Donald was besotted with the dog, as he was an animal lover. Lady had a good temperament, she was loyal, well behaved and highly intelligent as Jack Russell terriers are prone to be.

Although Donald had worked in Fish & Chip shops as a child, he wanted to experience the management element of the Fish & Chip shop business, so looked to see what could be done to gain this necessary experience. He had to see if he would be able to offer free employment to a takeaway establishment that was sufficiently distant from his own business premise. He did not want to compete and impair another business. Donald travelled outside the local catchment area, and he saw a Takeaway business that was operating on a fast moving busy road in the town of Ilminster.

He knocked on the door of the house attached to the business, as the shop door was closed. The door opened, and a dark haired lady, with a strong Irish accent asked what he wanted. She looked just like Mrs Doyle from the TV sitcom 'Father Ted'. Donald explained that he was intending to open a takeaway business a long distance from their own shop, and asked if he could work in their business, free of charge, just for the experience. She introduced herself as Sally, and invited Donald into the house. She then called for her husband, called Phil. Donald shook hands with Phil. He was a prematurely white haired middle aged Irish man. He had a Dublin accent, and the couple seemed very friendly. They had three young children, and had come to the United Kingdom to try out a new career in the Fish & Chip trade. They accepted Donald's proposition, and they soon all became very good friends. Phil and Sally were introduced to Penny and the children, and it wasn't before long that the two families spent a lot of social time at each other's homes.

Phil's shop was a massive building, which also incorporated a public bar area, as it used to be a licensed premises operating as both a bar and a takeaway. However, Phil was just using the shop as a business and the bar room was an empty space.

Donald took an interest in all that Phil was doing to making a success of his business. The cooking range was archaic and really difficult to cook from. The extraction vent from the range did not have sufficient flow, and the fumes would blow back into the face of the fryer. So Phil's face appeared permanently flushed when he was hunched over the range. Donald also noted that Phil spent an inordinate time peeling the potatoes, and not leaving any 'eyes' at all in the potatoes. The potatoes looked perfectly clean and white. It seemed to Donald that too much of the potato itself was being rumbled away, which meant that profits were being rumbled away in the same direction of the potatoes.

Phil had indeed bought a business that was situated on a busy main road. Busy roads are usually good for businesses as a rule, but not so good if there is nowhere to park, and the road is a clearway where drivers are not allowed to stop. So, in this case potential customers just sped by.

There appeared to be many inconsistencies that Donald noticed with the way Phil ran the business, and he tried to make useful suggestions to Phil in an attempt to reduce the labour and improve his profit margin. But Phil, who was older that Donald by around eleven years, thought Donald not to be sufficiently experienced to give any positive advice.

This did not affect their relationship, as Donald was enjoying working at the shop he could fine tune the knowledge gleaned in order that he could use it wisely, and make his own business as successful as possible. Phil was giving incredibly good value for the food, as they were the cheapest fish and chips for miles around. Donald was concerned, as there seemed to be very little working profit, which may jeopardise the health of the business.

One morning at around 10am and before the shop opened for business. A local businessman who was selling carpets, had stopped on the double lines outside of the shop. He shouted through the open window that he had some bargain carpets in the back for sale. Donald looked at Sally, who in turn looked to Phil, who was busy cleaning the range. "You two go and have a look if you want!" he said, and then turned back to the range and his cleaning job. Donald and Sally stepped out onto the sunny pavement, and peered into the back of the van at the assortment of rolled carpets.

Donald, who was in a flirtatious mood said to Sally "Look Sally, wouldn't that carpet look lovely in our bedroom!" pointing at one particular carpet. Before Sally could answer, the salesman said to Sally "Don't you think you should ask your Dad first, pointing in the direction of Phil, who was still hunched over his range. Sally let out a ripping laugh at the suggestion. They returned together into the shop chuckling together. Sally told her husband that the salesman thought that she and Donald were married and that Phil was her father. Phil was not amused. He kept repeating "Her dad, her dad, that's my wife!"

On another occasion, when Phil wanted to revamp the abandoned lounge that was once the general bar. He had hired a carpenter to carry out the task of updating some of the woodwork. Phil suggested bat wing doors that would swing open and closed for easy access. The carpenter agreed, and said that it should be a simple procedure. He then set about working on the aperture and adding the doors. Regrettably the outcome was not really perfect. The doors did swing, but they only swung out at an awkward angle, and they also hung at different lengths. The carpenter did the best he could. Donald had watched him from the kitchen as he struggled with the job. It was indeed and impediment, that although his right arm was fine, he did not have a left arm, as it had been amputated at the shoulder!

It was now time for Donald's temporary employment with Phil and Sally to come to an end as Donald's own shop was just a few short weeks away to completion.

He had booked a five day training course with a training company in Grimsby that specialised in teaching people the theory and practice of fish frying. To the lay person it would appear that there would not be a lot to learn. But like everything else, something that looks easy, in practice it is not. This was the same with the five day course. Donald was amazed at what was involved, the type of fish and the difference between Norwegian cod and Icelandic cod. Cooking methods, oil changes, temperatures, storage, ordering and the many little nuggets of information that would ensure an improved chance of success for any budding fish & chip shop proprietor and manager.

When Donald was having a drink one lunchtime in a local pub, he lapsed into conversation with a stranger at the bar. They chatted about things in general, and then the subject matter came around about fish & chip businesses, and what would make a successful takeaway. The stranger made a point, laughing and saying that some idiot had bought the shed in the village of Lyng, and was turning it into a chip shop. Donald gave it a second or two and responded "That idiot is me!" There was no bad feeling with the stranger at the bar, as Donald chuckled about the exchange later, but his resolve was strengthened in that he would make a success of the business, come hell or high water!

The Fish and Chip shop had been refurbished to a high standard. He thought it novel to name the shop 'Donald's Plaice'. Douglas Plodd, Donald's previous boss had volunteered to fund the artwork for the Shop signage which was very generous of him.

The new shop now had concrete block walls, a tiled roof. Wooden cladding to the front elevation. It had been extended, and had a decent shop space, a preparation room, a lobby leading to a toilet with washbasin. The second hand range gleamed. There was a cold drinks cabinet, shelving, microwave oven, griddle, pizza grill and even a small TV to entertain waiting customers. There was also a breakfast bar running along one wall with three stools for any clients who wished to eat their food inside the shop.

The preparation room was light and airy, with a potato rumbler, an electric shipper machine, a domestic sink and draining board, and two fridge freezers.

Donald sourced the appropriate wholesalers for frozen Icelandic fish. Cash and Carry wholesalers were utilised for sundries, and local suppliers for Maris Piper potatoes, the best chipping potatoes. Donald realised that as the shop was not in a prime location, he would have to offer customers a higher standard and a more extensive menu in order to attract clientele from a greater radius.

Beyond the standard choice of fish, sausages, chicken portions, mushy peas, curry sauce etc. Donald offered a choice of pizza toppings, freshly made burgers, chicken and beef curries. For the nights of Thursday, Friday and Saturday, these would be special nights, and customers would be offered a special dish of the week, which could be stroganoff, chop suey, chow mein and other dishes of speciality. This initiative in time generated a real interest with customers, who would ring in and ask "What's the special this week?" It reminded Donald of the 'red spot' menu's that he had introduced on-board ships years before. Menus were printed for distribution to homes in the district, and Donald added at the bottom of each printed menu *'Every Meal a Banquet'*. As this was the exact phrase used by Donald's previous adversary, Paddy, the Chief Engineer that had needled him for a four month voyage. The Chief Engineer proved that he has his uses by giving Donald a good idea for his menu presentation.

Donald had advertised the opening of the new business in the local newspapers. There were acknowledgements to the various tradesmen and businesses involved with the refurbishment, and so all was ready for the grand opening. Donald's wife Penny offered her help behind the counter along with a young girl from the village, hired as an assistant. Donald provided a smart uniform where staff, including himself, would wear white trilby hat's with a band of red ribbon. The ladies would wear a tabard and bib apron, and Donald would wear a red jacket and bib apron. Front of house would look smart and professional. Upon opening the door, there would be a long queue of customers that snaked from the shop, along the pavement and fifty yards up the road. There were a lot of people who were curious, as with any new business, to see the transformation that Donald had made from a building that was initially a shed, and then transforming it into a modern fish and chip takeaway. The opening night was a tremendous success. Though Donald realised that the opening night was really the easy bit, the real work, was how to maintain a good flow of consistent custom, in order for the business to survive and thrive.

The business proved to be very hard work, as with anything, hard work, consistency and dedication are the hall marks of any successful enterprise. Donald worked a six day week. He was not allowed to work on a Sunday due to being a British national and the Sunday trading laws of the day. However, a six day week was a challenge. He would arrive at the shop in the morning, to prepare fish, then peel the potatoes, prepare the curry dishes for refrigeration, make the homemade fish cakes, and prepare the baked bean fritters for the freezer. Making sure that the shop was spotless before opening for the lunch period. He would take two hours off in the afternoon, before returning to the shop for the tea-time opening which extended to 10.30pm for three days a week, and a midnight closing on Thursday, Friday and Saturday for the pub trade.

The business gradually increased its turnover. Donald realised that his profit margins were under par with regard to other take-away businesses, which were in better locations, such as towns with large public car parks close to their businesses. However, he also realised that he had to offer a product that was different to the norm in order to attract more custom.

Staff, like any business come and go, and Donald would advertise for staff in the local newspapers. Some that were employed were good, and some were not so good. Donald employed one young lad, who, when he was serving customers, could not grasp basic arithmetic skills, and although the shop had an electronic till register, the lad would grab at the customers proffered bank note, without really knowing what the full cost of the meal totalled, and what change was required in return. Needless to say, he didn't last too long. Another staff member was a lady in her thirties, who was very easy on the eye, though she had a blond hair-do that seemed to extend around a foot from the circumference of her head, which made Donald dodge her hair-do as he passed her behind a narrow counter. She looked good, but she was another recruit that had no idea how to serve customers with their basic needs.

Another young lad that lasted a couple of weeks, was OK with his duties, but preferred out-door activities. It was summer, and during a busy frying session, Donald noticed the lad was sweating profusely. The young man, on one occasion, swayed on his feet, saying to Donald "I don't feel well, I think I'm going to faint!" Donald, who was busy frying fish, looking sideways at him, and said "Well you can't! There's not enough room!"

Donald enjoyed the rapport that he had with his customers. He believed that if you have to be busy serving people, you also have to enjoy the experience, and also make the customers enjoy coming to your shop. So there had to be a sense of good humour, genuine friendliness along with good quality fare. Customers had to see that Donald and staff were friendly and welcoming. So there were lots of laughs and banter between Donald and his customers. This appealed to customers, they at least where entertained, whilst they waited their turn for service in the queue.

Customers ranged from the very poor to the very rich, and Donald appealed to all ranges. The knack was to quickly gauge the personality and pitch the conversation accordingly.

Across the road from the shop lived a family called the Lancelot's. A poor family, that were not particularly well educated, and with social problems in regard to personal hygiene. The father was a little man in his sixties, his wife Molly was a woman with a toothless grin. They had two sons in their twenties, one called Norman and other called Les. Both lads were frequent visitors to the shop. They were amiable chaps, well behaved and courteous. Though they did emit a problematic body odour that was sometimes very over powering in the small shop space, especially on a hot day. They used to wear the same blue boiler-suits, but the problem lay in that the boiler-suits obviously never left their bodies, and were dirty smelly. If Norman or Les turned up at the back of a queue, then they were given 'special treatment' where Donald would quickly bring them to the front of the queue, serve them quickly and let them leave the shop. In their eyes, this fast track service was brilliant.

Another local customer was a lady in her sixties called Mrs Edwards. She had a wayward son called Malcolm. She was on the poverty line, trying to exist on her social security hand-outs. Donald always tried to be kind and generous to Mrs Edwards. So when she turned up one evening at the shop, looking tired, pale and cold. Donald remarked to her that she did not look well. Mrs Edwards said "Well, I've no coal for the fire, and Malcolm is back in jail again!" Donald felt sorry for her predicament, so he gave her a free fish & chip supper. He then opened the till and brought out a five pound note, handing it to Mrs Edwards saying "For God's sake Mrs Edwards, take this, and buy yourself a bag of coal!" Mrs Edwards grabbed the banknote with thanks, and picking up her free fish supper, she scurried from the shop.

On another day, Mrs Edwards came into the shop, and Donald was shocked to see that her hair was no longer white, but a fluorescent electric blue! "What have you done there, Mrs Edwards?" Donald enquired. Mrs Edwards said "Ah, well I put the dye on, and I thought it would turn out brown, but I don't know what went wrong, and it turned out this colour!" "Well it has certainly brightened you up Mrs Edwards!" said Donald.

The same lady was in the queue one day, when she had the cheek to ask Donald for two sausages, and asked what were the chips were like, as they had not very nice when she had bought chips the day before. There was a long queue behind Mrs Edwards awaiting their turn. Donald was stunned that Mrs Edwards was being so picky. So he said to her in a raised voice, in order that everyone in the shop could hear the exchange. "The chips are horrible Mrs Edwards, I wouldn't have them if I were you!" Mrs Edwards, responded "Well I'll try them anyway." "No,No,No said Donald, you really don't, they're awful!" "Here you go, here are the sausages you wanted". He wrapped up the sausages, whilst Mrs Edwards stood speechless, handing them to her and taking her money. She left the shop muttering and growling. The customers in the queue, looking stunned, with a mixture of incredulity and bemusement.

Thirteen months after the shop had opened for business. The night was a Wednesday, and it was 30th December. Donald had a reasonable busy day at the shop, and at 10.30pm that night, he cleaned up and locked up the shop. He climbed into his van for the short journey of around a mile to his home. He was worn out, and was looking forward to a little nip of Whisky to help him unwind when he arrived to the warmth of his home. Donald went into the front room, and as usually, Penny was still up, awaiting his arrival. She had recorded the soap episode of 'Brookside', so that she and Donald could sit together and watch the soap. Donald grabbed himself a whisky from his cocktail bar in the lounge. He made Penny a cup of tea, as she really didn't like alcohol. They sat together and played the video recording and sat back to watch the soap. Donald was unwinding, feeling comfortable, nice and relaxed. He decided to have a second whisky and sat back sipping from his favourite whisky glass.

All of a sudden, there was someone frantically banging on the front door. Donald got up and opened it. The caller was the farmer who owned the farm opposite the chip shop. "Your chip shop's on fire!" he yelled at Donald. The farmer told him that the fire engine was already in attendance. Without a second thought, Donald thanked him, and shutting the door, he called to Penny and told her that the shop was on fire. He then got into his van and drove down the hill to the chip shop. On his approach, he saw the fire engine and the flashing lights. There were flames coming out of the shop windows and the firemen were busy hosing the shop down. Donald stopped the van in the street. He got out and made his way nearer to the shop. A Policewoman approached him with the tray of the cash register in her hands. She faced Donald, and asked him "Are you the proprietor?" "Yes, I am!" said Donald, forgetting that he had just drank two large whiskies, and the poor Policewoman reeled back as the whisky fumes hit her full in the face.

Donald was thankful that she had not arrested him on a drink drive charge.

The firemen had distinguished the fire, Chief Fire Officer had deemed it safe to enter the building. Donald followed them into the shop. His first worry was that the fire was of his own making, inasmuch that he had not switched the frying range off successfully, and the oil had over heated which in turn had caused the ultimate fire. However, a fireman examined the range, and it was confirmed that the range had been switched off safely. Upon further inspection, there were charred remains of a paper calendar, together with the singed remnants of Donald's apron. The evidence suggested that the apron and calendar had been ignited, and then thrown into the oil pan, which started the fire. The case was confirmed as arson. Donald was relieved that the fire was not of his own making, but he was angered to know that someone had felt that they had to break down the back door with deliberation and then set fire to his shop.

The police conducted an investigation, looking for any witnesses to the arson attack. The result was that neighbours had indeed seen two young men, running out of the shop after the fire erupted. The neighbours had then rang for the Police and the Fire Service. Although the perpetrators where identified as the possible arsonists, there was insufficient proof that they had actually started the fire, although they were seen running from the shop. A little incredulous, though that is the way of the law. Nobody was brought to justice for this crime.

Donald contacted his insurance firm and reported the crime. His broker called him to say that their insurance loss adjustor would contact him. However, before his arrival, a firm of insurance assessors contacted Donald and wanted to talk to him. Donald did not know the difference between a loss adjustor and a loss assessor. Though it was not before long that he was fully aware of the disparity.

A gent arrived, who was the insurance assessor, and met with Donald, telling him that as he held a new for old policy, for a small fee, they would represent his claim, that all of the repair, together with brand new industrial catering equipment would be installed into his shop with the insurance company footing the bill. This sounded fair to Donald, who then signed an agreement with their firm.

However, when Donald rang his insurance broker, and informed him of his meeting with the insurance assessor, the broker immediately broke into a sweat, and told Donald that he should have had nothing at all to do with them, as they were a bunch of sharks. Donald informed the broker from where he was standing, that they all looked like a pack of sharks. If Donald had not signed with the assessors, and had met with the loss adjustor (who worked in the best interest of the insurance company rather than the customer) they would have down sized the cost of repairs and refurbishment, and therefore Donald would not have had such a good deal.

The assessors that Donald had hired were true to their word, and for a small fee, they achieved the very best financial outcome for Donald. The insurance company would pay for the full refurbishment and repair of the shop. There would be a new cooking range, costing £10,000.00, there would be a new industrial catering microwave oven, a new griddle and new pizza grill. Industrial fridges and freezers, and industrial sink with draining board were also included and other benefits. Although Donald was initially angry that his shop had been set on fire, it really was a blessing in disguise, as he now would have an even better shop than before.

When he was inspecting the initial damage to the premises. The lovely old folk who lived near the vicinity of the shop would approach Donald, and with false concern, would tut, shaking their heads sadly, and say "Oh dear, isn't it awful, I suppose you're finished now, aren't you?" Donald would look at them calmly, and say "No, not at all, I'm insured, and lucky old you will have a nice new fish & chip shop again!" Donald enjoyed looking at the undisguised disappointment in their faces. He put this down to a small village mentality, where it was easy to feel envy for someone else who was trying to make a go of a business, someone who was trying to better themselves and be a success for themselves and their family, whilst providing local people with a fast food outlet on their doorstep.

The shop fire generated a lot of publicity. The news story and film footage showed on the BBC West news, and Donald was interviewed by other TV stations and local newspapers. Donald found it puzzling that people from miles around would make their way to the village and drive slowly past the shop, whilst having a good eyeful of the damage and debris. Well, at least the shop was now on the map.

It was around eight weeks of refurbishment and the instalment of new equipment before Donald could re-open his business again. Donald decided to change the hours of opening. He wanted to concentrate more on the family trade, rather than the pub clientele. The shop would now close at 10.30pm every night. Therefore avoiding the pub clientele, mostly drunken young men, who came in for a spring roll and curry sauce, and usually created mayhem! Whereas the family trade was far more lucrative. People buying food for the entire family paid much better dividends.

The shop re-opened and trade increased by another 30%. Whenever clients from the pub trade came in, and looked like they may cause trouble. Donald would lift a heavy wooden cudgel that he had purchased on a previous ship visit to Cape Town, and slam the truncheon down on the stainless steel counter with a loud bang. That usually got the message across, that there would be no trouble coming from drunken yobs.

A year following the fire. Donald's fiancée Penny announced that she was pregnant. This was great news for Donald, as although he already had two lovely children, there was enough room for another. Donald's mother and father, Walter and Margo were thrilled with the news. They would sometimes make the journey from Bangor to Somerset to visit Donald and his family. Walter, had by now become a man of religion. Although he had also been an elder at the church for years, he longed to preach from the pulpit. He was a fervent churchgoer, and Donald remembered as a child that he, together with Ronald, and his sister Elsie were usually frogmarched to church every Sunday. Walter in his spare time was now a lay preacher, and enjoyed gesticulating his sermon from the pulpit, even if most of the pews were vacant. So when Walter visited in Somerset and stayed with Donald and the family. Walter would settle down and read fervently. Donald asked him once "What are you reading then, Dad?" "Prayers for the Busy Man" Walter responded. Donald would roll his eyes, and let him carry on.

Margo's health was going steeply into decline. She could no longer sit up, and could not lie in a bed. She had developed curvature of the spine, and sat nearly doubled up with her chin on her chest. She had been wearing a foam neck brace, though she found that the restraint caused her discomfort, so she made Walter whittle the foam further and further, reducing the width, until only a thin strip encased her neck, which did nothing to help her condition. She also was accumulating excessive water in her legs, and leg ulcers were a permanent condition. Walter used to bathe them with a zinc concoction, but they never improved.

In September Penny was nearing the end of her pregnancy, and one Wednesday afternoon she went into labour, so Donald rushed her to Taunton Hospital. Penny's parents came over to look after Belinda and Archie. This would the first night that the shop would not open. They arrived at the hospital in good time, and Penny was taken to the maternity Suite.

Donald stayed with her and endeavoured to comfort her. It was a new experience for him, and so he wasn't sure that he was much use at all in this situation. However, he was doing his best.

The labour took really a long time, and a baby girl was born at 1.25 am the next morning. She was beautiful, and Donald was the first to hold his little bundle of joy. The nurse asked if anyone wanted a sandwich, and brought some into the ward. Penny was not feeling hungry, but the effort and strain had worn Donald out. It had left him ravenous, and he ate all the sandwiches with great gusto.

After staying with Penny and the baby for an hour, Donald left them both so that they could both rest. On the way home in the dark at around 3am, a cat ran out in front of Donald's car, though it luckily escaped the wheels of the car. Donald sighed with relief. This was short lived, as another cat who had been chasing the first cat, was less fortunate, and was struck by Donald's car. Death was instant. Donald continued the journey home along empty roads, then behind him he saw the flashing lights of a police car, which was flagging him down. The policemen got out of their vehicle and asked Donald what he was doing. Donald asked if he had been speeding, and the police said they had a hard job keeping up. Donald was unsure if they were joking. They had actually stopped him out of sheer boredom. Donald explained that his partner had just given birth to their baby girl, and that he was on his way home. The policemen congratulated Donald and let him go on his way.

They decided to call their baby girl Felicity, well the name did rhyme with Penelope. Felicity and Penny arrived home a day after the birth. The first visitors to see the baby, came from surprise travellers all the way from Bangor. Donald's sister Elsie, and her husband Frank. They cooed over baby Felicity. She had a mop of black hair, and in our eyes was the prettiest baby that we had ever seen. Belinda and Archie were happy to have a new baby sister, and they were good around the baby.

Donald and Penny remained good friends with Phil and Sally from the training chip shop. However, Phil's business had taken a nose dive. His clientele had dwindled and he was struggling to make ends meet. Phil used to sell onion bahjees in his shop, and he had a brain wave in how to make money. So he approached the wholesaler who made the bahjees, and paid the wholesaler £1,000.00 for the recipe. Donald found this a little strange, not that Phil wanted to make the bahjees, but the exorbitant price that he had paid for the recipe. Phil then bought a batch of six second hand chest freezers and slotted them into his shop space. He shut down the shop, and concentrated fully on making bags of bahjees, freezing them, with the intention of selling them to retail outlets. However, Phil had rushed into the project without any market research to establish if indeed there was a viable market for bahjees. And if sufficient profit could be made to provide an income. Phil's bahjees worked out at about five pence each, though they were purchased by the bag which contained around 30 bahjees. Donald bought a few bags from Phil, as he was Phil's friend, but he was concerned, no fortune could be made from this madcap enterprise.

Donald was right, though he would have preferred to have been wrong, as he liked Phil and Sally, they were good friends, and he just wished that they would eventually do well. Things went from bad to worse, the bahjee enterprise was basically a non-starter. Phil decided to sell his house and his business.

In order for Phil to encourage the sale of his business and entice prospective buyers, convincing them that the business was worth buying. He devised a plan to use two accounts books. One with the actual sales figures and the meagre profit margin, and a second book that showed inflated sales with a healthy profit. The shop and business was eventually sold, but to a private buyer that was turning the building into private apartments, rather than using it as a viable takeaway business. The business sold for under the market price for a quick sale. Phil, though was pleased, as the business had become a yoke around his neck. The not so good news was that as he had used the second book with the inflated sales figures showing the healthy profit. Phil had already declared these figures in his end of year Tax return. So he paid VAT on sales that were never actually made!

Phil decided to rent a fully furnished house in Taunton. It was a nice semi-detached property in a good part of town. Raymond managed to find work with a removal company, and used their van for home use. He wanted to reverse the van into the driveway where his car was parked, as there was sufficient room for two vehicles on Phil's drive. On this occasion, he reversed the van, but misjudged the turn, and the van slammed into the street lamp on the pavement, which then toppled toward Phil's Audi saloon, hitting the car flat bang on the roof before continuing to slam onto the bonnet.

This was an unfortunate accident, as the car was a write-off. However, Phil would have none of it, and paid additional insurance to have the vehicle completely renovated.

Phil then made plans to open a franchise café at a local swimming pool and leisure centre complex. He made plans for the new business, and hoped that he would receive the contract. The deal fell through, and the franchise was offered to another entrepreneur.

In his youth, Phil had lived and worked in London, and had run a successful ice cream business, driving on a round in an ice cream van making a good living.

Phil was now struggling to know how he could turn his fortunes around, so he decided that he would move his wife and family to London. This was an unusual decision, as it was during the period when Mrs Thatcher's Government made the sale of council houses possible for sitting tenants. This suited tenants of properties in London and the home-counties. It was soon realised that these tenants could sell their London homes for huge amounts of money, and then buy luxury properties in other counties such as Somerset. It was difficult to understand why Phil wanted to up sticks to London, when Londoner's were heading out of London in droves. Phil put an offer in for an ex council semi-detached three bedroomed house outside central London. He even upped his offer to over the asking price to ensure that the property would be his. Phil and his family bought the property and it was a new beginning. Phil then bought a second hand ice cream van, buying stock including sweets, crisps and soft drinks, and he set about driving the van looking for custom. He telephoned Donald to tell him how happy he was in his new enterprise, and told Donald "This is what it's all about, not like the chip shop were you waited for your custom. Here, you can be mobile and can find customers!" Phil invited Donald down for the day to experience his new business. Donald was pleased that Phil was doing well, and was keen to see his old friend again. Donald travelled down to London and met with Phil and Sally at their new home. After a while, Phil invited Donald to keep him company in the van as he went on his rounds. Donald donned a white coat and hat, and sat in the back of the van whilst Phil drove the vehicle, turning on the microphone which played out the 'Teddy Bears Picnic'. He would stop on an empty street, and a little Indian lad would turn up and Phil would slide open the glass partition, and ask the little lad what he would like. "Please can I have a strawberry gob stopper?" the lad asked. "Of course you can!" Phil said as he reached into a jar and took out a gob stopper handing it to the boy. "That will be threepence please" Phil told the boy. He paid up and ran off. "That's the way to do it Donald!" Phil said. He then climbed back into the driver's seat in search of new custom. Donald sat in the back, still a little bewildered at the last transaction. Donald was thinking of the cost of diesel for this little adventure. By the end of a four hour shift, they returned back to the house. Phil had made £4.52pence for an afternoon's work.

Donald left them that evening and wished them both well as he travelled back to Somerset.

During the following months Phil kept in touch with Donald, and told him that the ice cream trade had changed since his younger days as a salesman. The trade was now sewn up with mafia guarded sales routes for only those allowed a piece of the action. Unfortunately Phil was not part of this particular union, and the other ice cream vendors where not happy that this interloper was trying to muscle in on their patches. Phil was warned off, but ignored the threats, and continued trading in areas that caused friction with the other vendors.

As Phil's ice cream van was parked in the back lane behind his house, with the electrics plugged in under his garage door to keeping the ice cream frozen, it was vulnerable to vandalism. Phil would have preferred that the van could have been stored in his garage, but the roof was too low to incorporate the van. One evening, Phil topped up the van with ice cream, ice lollies, sweets, crisps and soft drinks, and the van was parked behind his home in the usual spot ready for business the following morning. Next day, Phil went to his van to start his round, to find that the van had been broken into and all of his stock had been stolen. This was terrible news. He told Donald of this tragedy, and Donald was upset for Phil, and said "Well, at least you were insured! And you can get the money back!" Phil replied, saying "But, I'm not insured!" There was not much else to say on the matter.

Phil paid to have the roof raised on his garage, so that the van could be safe indoors and off the road. Though the damage was now done, and he knew that he could not win against the ice cream mafia.

He sold the van and bought a VW taxi. He was a good driver and navigator. He did quite well in the business. However, when he decided to sell the car, he tried to scam a potential buyer, by asking a mechanic to put the mileage gauge back by 40,000 miles. For a back-hander, the mileage was reduced accordingly. A potential buyer expressed an interest in the vehicle, and asked if he could take it for a test drive on his own, whilst leaving his own vehicle at Phil's house as a guarantee. This was agreed, and the buyer went for the test drive. However, unbeknown to Phil, the prospective buyer stopped the car a few miles up the road. He inspected the car, and upon opening the glove box, he located the vehicle service record book. Upon examination of this document, he noticed an anomaly. He saw the last date of service, and the mileage gauge record showing over 120,000 miles, and when he checked the mileage on the vehicle it only showed 80,000 miles on the clock. He returned the car back to Phil, asking him why the vehicle was 40,000 miles short of the actual figure. Phil was stuck for words, as he knew that the game was up. It was a shortcoming of Phil that he never thought a plan out through thoroughly enough. Donald was a little peeved with Phil, as he was the instrument of many of his misadventures. He did tell Phil, that altering the mileage in a vehicle was a criminal offence, and he could end up in jail for fraud.

There were more stories that followed for Phil, and his fortune never improved. It was a pity, as he was a good man, just a very poor businessman.

The fish and chip business turnover had reached its peak, and it was unlikely to improve, although the profit sustained Donald and his family with a steady and reasonable income. So around two years following the birth of baby Felicity, Donald decided to put the business on the market. Donald had managed to pay off the original bank loan against the business. He had also paid off the mortgage from his home, so all money from the sale of the business, could be reinvested. Donald managed to sell the shop for £50,500.00. In those days that was quite a sizeable sum of money. He did not want the money to be frittered away, so he decided to reinvest the cash back into property. He purchased a small semi-detached two bedroom cottage in the village of Milverton for £29.950.00. He furnished the property, and rented it out for £300 a month to a newly married couple. As Penny's parents, who also lived in Milverton, were tenants in their council house that they had lived in for over forty years. They were entitled to buy this large three bedroom semi-detached property with a small front garden and an extremely large back garden. The local council were contacted, and a deal was agreed that Penny's parents could purchase the house from the council for the sum of £9,000.00. Donald gave Danny & Gwen a cheque for £9,000.00 and they became the proud owners of their own home, and were no longer accountable to pay rent.
Donald now felt pleased that the hard work through the years with his own business had paid off, and the money had been reinvested wisely. He could now think were his career would take him next.
As he had always been happy at sea, for the majority of the time. He searched to see what employment was still available for a British national. The shipping world had changed in the six years since he had been at sea, and the number of positions for British nationals to serve in the Merchant Navy was now drastically reduced.
Donald was unsure on which course his career would now take. So he considered that there may be an opportunity to work on-board one of the many oil rigs operating in the North Sea. The only way a person could apply for this type of work was if they were holders of the off shore safety certificate. He had to gain this certificate, and would have to pay the course funds himself, without sponsorship.

Donald looked up the details of available courses, and for a charge of £1,100.00 plus accommodation expenses, Warsash College in Southampton held the sea survival course involving life rafts, and a college in Great Yarmouth offered the second part of the course, which involved the simulated helicopter crash course.

Donald applied for both courses, and paid the course fees. The courses were set over a period of five days. He travelled down to Southampton for the sea survival course which involved jumping into a swimming pool from one of the diving boards, and then swimming to a life raft and scrambling aboard without assistance from other course members. Donald had undertaken the course years before, when he was much fitter, and the course was easier because he had been a lot younger. Now that he was in his late thirties and carrying a few extra pounds, struggling to heave himself into the life raft unaided, proved a mighty struggle. With a lot of heaving, and panting, he eventually hauled himself out of the water, landing in a crumpled mass in the well of the raft. Donald passed the course, then set off for the second challenge in Great Yarmouth. There was a class of around fifteen men of varying ages on the course. Donald was one of the oldest in the group. They were all led into an indoor swimming pool area, and looking upward on a hoist was a simulated fuselage of a helicopter. The name of the game was that they would board the helicopter, and take their allocated seats. They would then all take a deep breath, holding it, whilst the helicopter was dropped into the water from a long cable, the helicopter would then capsize under the water, and then divers in wet suits and breathing apparatus, would tap each person on the shoulder, where they would then unbuckle their seat belt whilst upside down in their seats, and then try to make their way to the exit door, and up to the surface of the pool. Sounds easy! Not so. Donald like all the others, assembled inside the craft and buckled up. The craft was lowered at a great rate of knots, and Donald just managed to take a breath of air, before the water quickly came over his head. The experience reminded him instantly of his bath time experiences as a child, and Walter's water-boarding techniques. That awful feeling of drowning. Donald fought to keep calm. He felt a tap on his shoulder, and unbuckling his belt, went in the wrong direction, but was steered by the diver to the open door, and out of the craft, where Donald swam to the top, gasping and spluttering. If only that was the end of the experience, but it wasn't.

The procedure was implemented for a second turn. Other course members were of a mix in their enjoyment of the procedure. Most did not like it at all, and even an experienced diver agreed that holding your breath in those particular circumstances, was both difficult and harrowing. One guy on the course after the second attempt, refused to go back for the third and final attempt. The course instructors warned him that should he refuse to go back for the final dip, then he would not be able to gain the certificate. He said "Bugger the certificate!" and walked off the course. The third attempt was the worst, as Donald on this occasion was told that he would be sitting at the back of the craft, and he would be the last one to leave, and had to wait for the pat on the back, before attempting to leave his seat. All went well, and Donald kept holding his breath. The time seemed to be an eternity, and then he felt the tap on his back. He went to unbuckle his seat belt, but found that he could not release the clasp. There was a second tap on his back, and Donald nodding furiously, as he struggled with the belt buckle. Panic was creeping in at an alarming rate, and then, with a clunk, he released the belt, and with great relief was guided out of the craft and up to the surface of the pool. Gulping in air and happy to be alive. Donald received his hard earned certificate. But it had all been for nothing, as Donald could not find a vacancy in the catering department with any oil rig company. Well, it was an experience.

Donald resumed his search for employment. Texaco Tankers still had two vessels that maintained a full British crew of officers and ratings.

Figure 1 Walter and Margo

Figure 2   The Cottage at Llangogog

Figure 3   From Left: Donald, Elsie, Ronald

Figure 4 Sea School 1967 -Donald standing on left of picture

SHELL TANKER s.s. "ALINDA" 18.317 d.w. tons.

Figure 5 Shell Tankers

Figure 6 Donald and Singaporean pals

Figure 7   Donald promoting British & Thai Diplomacy

Figure 8   Donald & Penny at Don's Plaice

Figure 9   From Left: Belinda, Archie, Flick

Figure 10 Shop Before rebuild

Figure 11 Shop after rebuild

CHAPTER ELEVEN
BACK ON THE OCEAN WAVE

Donald had to renew his National Union of Seaman card, and take another medical to be accepted back at sea. There was a vacant position on a ship called the MV Windsor, a Texaco Tanker. The position was that of a Second Cook and Baker, a rank that Donald had held many years previously, and well down the pecking order from the position of Catering Officer. However, Donald was a pragmatist, and no longer could think of himself as too good for a lowly position, so he accepted their offer of employment and set about his return to a sea-going career. This was certainly a wrench in having to leave his family. He had been enjoying family life. A loving fiancée, three beautiful children, and of course Lady, his Jack Russell terrier. The decision was not an easy one to make, but in order to provide for his family, and backed by his own self-belief of success he considered that the return to sea was the best option. He signed a contract with Texaco for a four month trip. Joining the vessel in the port of Stanford Le Hope, a port in the London area.

It did not take long for Donald to adjust to the role of second cook & baker. It was like riding a bike, once mastered, you never forgot. He worked alongside a Chief Cook and Galley Boy. Donald noticed that the Officers thought a lot of themselves, and the British ratings were a militant bunch who totally believed in the role of the trade unions, and made sure that they worked to rule. Anyway, he settled into his job, and for two months there were no issues. Then came the news that on the other vessel owned by Texaco with a full British crew, called the MS Westminster that their Chief Cook had suffered a heart attack, and had to sign off the ship as a medical emergency. As maritime law dictated that the vessel could not sail without a crew member holding the Part 2 Cookery Certificate. Donald held a part 1, part 2, and also a Higher Grade Cookery certificate, and also Head of Department certificate, so he was well over qualified for the promotion. He was signed off, and transferred to the MV Westminster, taking the position of Chief Cook for a two month period.

Donald joined the vessel successfully, noticing that Officers and ratings were similar to the crew on-board the sister ship. The menus were A La Carte for both Officers and ratings, and the standard of catering was extremely high. The Catering Officer on-board, was in Donald's opinion an ineffective man. He was nearing retirement and in fact due to resign in the following two months. He was out of touch with reality, and cocooned in his self-importance. Donald had seen many people like him before. In order that another Catering Officer was ready to replace this old gent, a young bespectacled dork of a guy was on-board in a training capacity, signing on as a Junior Catering Officer. The young fella seemed to be quite bright in technical terms, but gangly and impractical in physical terms. He followed the older Catering Officer around like a lap dog, nodding sagely whenever his elderly superior gave professional opinions on how to run the catering department successfully. Donald watched this mismatched couple with silent bemusement. They were aloof and distant with Donald, they obviously considered Donald to be a disruptive influence. One day the senior catering officer came into the galley and informed Donald that his protégé would be making the dessert, as that his speciality signature dish was Lemon Meringue Pie. Donald had no problem with this at all, and when the young chap came into the galley to begin his work of art, Donald made him welcome, whilst keeping an eye on him. The gawky young officer, clad in a spotless white bib apron got to work, mixing his pastry ingredients with methodical deliberation, rolling out the pastry with a military precision. He baked the pastry 'blind' in the approved manner. He then began the task of making the lemon curd filling, and all was going along splendidly. However, when he started to make the meringue, he whisked the egg whites, but when wanting to add the sugar, he went to the wrong container. Donald immediately tried to stop him, but the young man, who thought that Donald was well beneath him, and therefore irrelevant, told Donald to mind his own business. Donald sighed and left him to it. The end product looked marvellous and absolutely delicious. Though, when it came to serving this beautifully produced cuisine, it was soon apparent, that when officers cut the meringue with their dessert spoon and put it into their mouths, their taste buds were in for a nasty shock. The young junior catering officer had inadvertently mixed salt instead of sugar into the egg whites. Donald in his own defence, had tried to tell the officer that he was making a mistake, but he wouldn't listen. Both Senior and Junior Catering Officers were both miffed, but immune to their own incompetence. The Lemon Meringue was scratched from the menu, and replaced with Ice Cream.

It was now the run up to Christmas, and there was a mad flurry of activity in producing menus to celebrate Christmas Lunch. This was a time when twice a year, (Christmas Day & New Year's Day) that ratings were allowed to eat in the Officers saloon, and everyone was a big happy family.

As Donald was totally aware that since he had joined the vessel, the officers remained aloof at all times, and were unfriendly and unsociable to Donald or indeed any other rating. They were like dinosaurs, trapped in yesterday's world.

So when the big day came, and it was extremely busy in the galley, as Donald and his colleagues frantically prepared the cuisine to be presented to both officers and ratings, in the officers' dining room at lunchtime. Everything was managed with meticulous care, and the serving of the various courses by the stewards to the crew went magnificently. It was the usual custom at Christmas, the catering department would be invited into the dining room at the end of the meal, where the Captain would make a speech, and thank the catering department for the sumptuous meal, and then everyone would applaud loudly.

So when the desserts and coffees had been served, the Captain sent in the Third Engineer to summon the Chief Cook and his staff to come into the dining room for the customary applause. The Third Engineer jauntily entered the galley and stepping up to Donald, he said "Jolly nice lunch Chief Cook, jolly nice!" Donald looked up from his work, and unsmiling, said "What do you want?" "Well, to get you and the rest of the catering department to come into the dining room, so that the Captain can thank you all for the meal" replied the Third Engineer. Donald answered "Well, the others can troop in if they want, but I am staying here, thanks!" The Third Engineer, knowing that he had a mission to accomplish said "You have to come in, and I will stay here until you agree to come in!" "Well you've a long f*****g wait, haven't you?" Donald retorted. Donald then added "If you lot can be such ars*h***s throughout the year, then please don't take a day off, on my account, now piss off!"

With that the Third Engineer did an about turn and returned to the dining room to pass on the basics of the interaction to the Captain. The rest of the team went into the dining room, and from the galley, Donald heard the customary applause.

When a week later, the New Year's lunch was served. At the end of the meal, the Captain entered the galley and came up to Donald and said "I know that you won't come into the dining room. I just wanted to thank you for such a nice lunch." Donald put out his hand, and shook the Captain's hand, saying "Thank you Captain, very much appreciated, and let me wish you a sincere happy new year." The Captain smiled and thanked him, and asked if he would like to join him later that afternoon for a drink in his cabin. Donald agreed, as he respected the Captain, and he thought of him as a decent fellow.

The ratings who were by and large militant and fervent followers of their trade union, wanted to put forward their claim for increased wages, better conditions and lots of benefits. There was a meeting scheduled for all crew, who were active members of the NUS. As Donald was a member, he considered that he had every right to attend the meeting. He went along at the scheduled time, and sat with the others on the long sofa seats. The Bosun, surrounded by his team of AB's, stood and shouted at the gathering "Welcome Brothers, we are meeting to discuss how we the working classes can improve our wages, as we believe that we are worth it!" There were cheers from the massed group, and shouts of "Up the working class!" Donald sat mute, as it seemed a little puerile. Did they not know that the writing had been on the wall years ago, that these 'brothers' would soon be out of a job and replaced by foreign ratings. Shipping companies had realised that they could employ foreign crew who would work twice as hard as their British counterparts, and cost a fraction in wages. No one it appeared had informed this band of brothers, the reality of life in the British Merchant Navy. Donald listened quietly to the demands of the ratings, and the costs were indeed eye watering. Donald put his hand up to speak. The Bosun said "Go ahead Cook!" Donald stood and said to the crew "Your demands which include improved wages, bonuses, overtime, the extension of leave amounts to around a 60% pay rise!" "Don't you think that the company would give your demands a more positive consideration, if you moderated the wage increase to a much lower percentage?" This comment brought silence to the room, and the Bosun then stood up and said "Rubbish! Brothers we are worth much more, and we will fight to get what we want!" Donald realised that his prudence was wasted on this crowd, and shup up for the rest of the meeting.

A year later, both ships lost their British ratings and were swapped for Filipino crew.

At the end of the trip, Donald was asked if he would like to sign a company contract and stay with Texaco. Donald declined, though he did not know what he would do following his departure from

Texaco, but the thought of staying, was more frightening than leaving.

Donald returned home on leave, and was happy to be with his family, while he looked for more sea-going employment. Donald was pleased to be home again with Penny, the children and also their little dog, who was thrilled to see him again.

Penny & Donald set a date for their pending wedding and agreed that they would marry after Donald's next trip.

Donald scoured the merchant navy ads for new postings, and by luck, there was a position available as Cook/Steward on a ship called the PALACIO operating out of Singapore. The ship was a container vessel, and because she was only a small container ship, she was classed as a 'feeder class vessel'. This meant that she was best suited to transfer small numbers of containers, between Singapore, Semarang and Surabaya, which were ports in Indonesia. This ship consisted of ten British nationals, there was the Captain, Chief Officer, Second Officer, Chief Engineer, Second Engineer, Motorman, Bosun, two Abs and a Cook/Steward.

The job of the Cook/Steward meant that he was a one man band in the catering department. This suited Donald, as he had the relevant experience. He was responsible for cooking three meals a day. The purchasing and victualling of all food provisions, together with bonded stores and slopchest. The slopchest is in simple terms a shop for crew members to buy toiletries, stationery, sweets, crisps and soft drinks. The bonded stores was for cases of beer, spirits, cigarettes and tobacco.

Donald also had to look after the laundry requirements which meant a change of bedding for all crew once a week, and the dirty laundry had to be logged and bagged in readiness for a shore-side laundry company to collect, wash and iron and return same to the vessel.

He was responsible for the cleanliness of the galley, messroom, pantry and all the fridge/freezer spaces, so he was kept busy a lot of the time.

Donald really enjoyed this position, as he could bake fancy bread and cookies. Arrange his menus, eliminate waste to the bare minimum, and keep the food cost to the daily company requirement by completing the victualling record accordingly. He was also responsible for crewing accounts from the purchase of sundries and bonded stores items.

The round trip involving the three ports was perfect, as the weather was always sunny, and Singapore was a brilliant run ashore, whilst Semarang and Surabaya were in contrast was part of a poorer country and not as disciplined as Singapore. Most crew stayed on the ship during the stay at the Indonesian ports, but Singapore was well worth waiting for.

The ratings although brilliant seafarers with tremendous experience found that they could cut corners when it came to graft. Donald used to see them in their cabins popping cans of lager, when they should have been on the deck. Donald queried why they had so little work. They said in unison "It's too hot on deck!" When on one occasion the ship deviated from the usual run of three ports, and sailed north to Japan where it was much cooler. Donald saw them together popping cans of lager, and queried again why they were not on deck "Too cold!" they said. It appeared that there was no happy medium to induce them to complete a full day's work.

The crew, Officers and ratings enjoyed Donald's cuisine, and he got on well with everyone on-board. It was novel for Donald to see that due to the size of the ship (2,500 tonnes DWT) there was only one dining room and this was for the entire crew, so good to see everyone eating together in one room.

J[Four months passed really quickly, and the Master sent word to the company bosses that Donald was very good at his job, and should be utilised more effectively. The company then offered Donald the position of Purser with their sister company called the Bank Line.

CHAPTER TWELVE
DONALD WEDS PENNY

Donald returned home for leave after his successful trip on the PALACIO. This was the leave that he and Penny would get married. After all they had been living together do over three years, and little Felicity who they now called 'Flick' was born, so it was time that the family became totally legitimised.

The local chapel at Pudding Well had been booked for a Saturday wedding. Brother Ronald had bought a house in the village Ilminster, he had married a few years earlier to a hot Latin Brazilian lady called Esmeralda, who was a divorcee with two grown up children. Donald helped Ronald with being accepted as a bar manager at the Ilminster Rugby Club. He bought a nice terraced cottage in the village, and Esmeralda was looking forward to life in the country, as she had lived an exciting life in Brazil and in London. Her previous husband had been a matador. Ronald was going to be Donald's best man at the wedding. Esmeralda would be matron of honour. Ronald was his usual self, he had never changed since childhood, laid back, charming and well liked. Esmeralda reminded Donald of his grandmother Fanny. Esmeralda liked the finer things in life, and had been an avid watcher of Dallas and Dynasty. Soaps that showed how the wealthy lived. Esmeralda wanted to be like her heroines with their trappings of wealth and frills. Her little terraced cottage was tiny, and she had her heart set on a four-poster bed. Whether the four-poster fitted or not, that was irrelevant. The bed was ordered from a very grand furniture store, and it was installed in their bedroom at the cottage. The only problem was that the bedroom door clanged against the bed when opened for slim access, which meant a really tight squeeze through the door and an acrobatic swivel of the body, to land upon the bed.

The day of the wedding arrived, and it was warm and sunny. Ronald and Donald waited at the front of the pews in the chapel. There was a good turn up for the wedding. Walter and Margo where there. Danny & Gwennie, then Meggie who was Penny's sister, and her brother Peter. Elsie and Frank had travelled down from Bangor. Archie was dressed in a white shirt, peach tie and grey suit. He was going to walk his mother down the aisle. Flick and Belinda were the beautiful bridesmaids. The bridesmaids wore dresses of peach and cream.

Penny walked down the aisle with Archie, and to the altar, then Archie sat with Nanny Gwennie in the seat next to her. Penny looked radiant. She was wearing a floral headdress, and a beautiful satin and lace ivory bridal gown.

The wedding was a triumph, and Donald & Penny exchanging their vows, were then pronounced husband and wife, and then they signed the register. Then hand in hand, they walked up the aisle and out into the sunshine. When the newlyweds were getting into the waiting car to take them to the reception, little Flick, pulled away from Nanny Gwennie and headed straight for the open door of the car, so that Donald and Penny had to bundle her in the back seat with them for the drive to the reception.

The reception was at the Horse & Hound Bar & Restaurant, a quaint Elizabethan establishment that catered for wedding events. The food was good and Ronald made a brilliant best man speech, and Donald was touched with Ronald's sensitivity, he had never noticed this quality in his brother before. Walter gave a speech, and said that marriage is a case of give and take, where he had given and Margo had taken. The joke raised a murmur of laughter. Poor Margo, who was sat in a wheelchair, knew where she was but was so incapacitated that Donald felt truly sorry for his mother and her predicament.

Now that Donald and Penny were married. They felt that the time was right to ensure a firmer family unity, as Belinda and Archie still retained the family name of their biological father. There was consideration on whether to change the surname to become double barrelled, but the family solicitor suggested that this was not the answer as the two children would still have a different name to their parents. The solicitor suggested placing their former surname into a middle Christian name, and if both Donald and Penny formally adopted the children, then all three children would all have the same legal status and also hold the surname of Drinkwater. This suggestion appealed to both Donald and Penny. Though of course before this could be finalised, the consent of the children was of paramount importance, and the final decision would be for the children to decide.

The family attended the family court, the judge was wearing his wig, as he had a pending trial case to attend, following his meeting with the Drinkwaters.

During the hearing the judge talked quietly to both Belinda and Archie, and asked them if they would like to be adopted, and if they had any objection to having their former surname changed into a middle Christian name. Both children spoke up and said that they happily accepted the change in name and their full agreement to being formally adopted by both parents. The judge smiled his acceptance, and thanked the children for their help and participation in the matter. Then young Flick who was also attending the court, although only three years old, she had been listening intently to the special attention that Belinda and Archie had received from the man in the wig. So after the judge had talked to both children, Flick shouted out at the friendly man in the wig "Can I be adopted as well?" The judge looked up at Flick, and smiling, said kindly "You don't need to be adopted, as you already have a loving mum and dad". Flick was not sure what he meant, as she thought that both Belinda and Archie had a loving mum and dad anyway. She still felt short changed.

So the new names were formalised. Archie was now, Archie Daniel Lewis Drinkwater, and Belinda was now Belinda Anne Lewis Drinkwater.

The Drinkwaters were now a family in every way possible, and they enjoyed like millions of others the unity, the love, the support and all the emotion that comes from parents striving to make life the very best for their children, and would not suffer the depravations and emotional turmoil, that they had themselves endured, during their own upbringing.

There were times when parenting was fun, and of course there were times, when it was exhausting. Whilst struggling with pressures of work on a day to day basis, coupled with worries for the future and employment prospects. It was paramount there was sufficient funds to bring up children with the feeling of self-belief, security and education, free-thinking and a positive ambition to succeed in the world.

Belinda was the best behaved child that any parent could ever wish for. She was smart, with a gentle nature, always willing to comply with any suggestion. She was quiet and studious. She enjoyed reading, and from an early age it was easily identified that she was very academic and hard working. She enjoyed achievement, and when she had reached one goal, she was already looking for the next challenge. Donald sometimes wished that he had done so much more for Belinda, as she was a sweet girl and she would grow up into a beautiful woman with so much love in her heart for everyone.

Archie, was like every other normal little boy. Self-absorbed with whatever he was doing at the time. Lost in fantasy as he played either with his dinosaur toys, or Thomas the Tank Engine, and his electronic game consoles. Donald was more severe with Archie than the girls. This, Donald thought at the time was because he wanted Archie to be prepared for the world outside, and to be in a well- placed position to manage the slings and arrows that were prolific in the adult world. This of course had to be balanced, as there was no way that he would treat Archie in a damaging upbringing as Walter had with Donald. This frightened Donald more than anything else. There were times when he had been totally unfair to the children, and it was during these times, that Donald would earnestly apologise to the children for his actions. The children would look at him bemused, and say that it was OK. However, any injustice played heavily on Donald's mind.

Archie and Belinda would go upstairs to their bedrooms around 8pm every night. Flick's bed was next to her parent's bed in the downstairs bedroom. Whilst Belinda went to her room, and was quiet for the rest of the night. Archie on the other hand was an insomniac, and really was a boy who was more alert at night. Many a night, he could be heard singing away in his soprano voice, sometimes drowning out the sound of the TV that Donald and Penny were watching. Donald would have to go up and see Archie and tell him to "Pipe down". Though after around ten minutes or so, he would start up again. He was a boy that did not let anything faze him.

He would then come out onto the landing and shout "I want to go the toilet!" He would then come down in his dressing gown and pyjamas, and with a cheeky smile would cross the living room in front of his parents and make his way to the bathroom. There was no way that Archie was not going to stop from being Archie!

Flick, the youngest was also a self-willed child. She was determined to last out for as long as possible before she could be put to bed, but Donald, who was totally blind, in that he could not help but love this girl to distraction. There was that innate fear that even the slimmest of chances, she would feel undermined by her parents, and grow up with unnecessary handicaps to overcome. Penny used to rebuke Donald for his ultra- lenient attitude when it came to Flick. She would say to Donald "You will rue the day for spoiling that girl!" Donald, as pig-headed as ever, took no heed of this sage advice. He just didn't want Flick or any of the children to experience anything similar to his own upbringing.

Flick soon picked up on who was the weakest link, and realised that she could play the situation to her own advantage. So every time Penny wanted to take control of Flick, the youngster would scream out "Daddy do it, Daddy do it!" Needless to say that there were some crossed words between Donald and Penny with regard to this infant. Donald did not see that his actions in spoiling the children during his short leaves at home would cause a headache for Penny when Donald had to return to sea. Penny had to bear the role of two parents, so there was no good cop, bad cop role play to enact. Penny was seen as the overall bad cop.

Due to the home being an old cottage, the only upstairs rooms where the two double bedrooms that could only be accessed by the steep narrow stairway in the lounge. The rear bedroom, looked over the back garden, and was on a higher elevation from the front bedroom, which looked out onto the main road. Donald was always concerned that in case of a fire in the cottage, then both Belinda and Archie could become trapped upstairs. So in order to manage this risk, Donald organised fire drills for the family. Donald would ring a bell, and the children would have to assemble outside the front door, as this was the allocated fire station. All three children were brilliant at the assembly, including Flick who thought that it was great fun. Donald then instructed Archie and Belinda and what action to take should they be trapped upstairs. He placed a small hatchet on a hook in the wardrobe of the front bedroom, and a rope ladder with instructions to break the glass in the front bedroom window, and hook the rope ladder over the sill, so that they could both climb down into the street. They were also instructed in how to stuff blankets at the foot of the bedroom door to limit in the ingress of smoke, and to stay low as there was more oxygen in the air at floor level. Donald was a safety freak, but considered safety and preparation where the best forms of defence in an emergency.

Donald had another fortnight's leave before he had to return to sea. He was looking forward to his first trip as Purser with the Bank Line.

The Bank Line had been a shipping company for over one hundred years with a fleet of six vessels.

The ships started out as general cargo, vegetable oil and container roll on-roll off ships. General cargo would be stored in the holds, with added tanks to hold the palm oil. The top decks would then be filled with containers. Throughout the century the ships had served the South Pacific Islands with produce from Europe, so anything from chocolate to JCB's and vehicles could be shipped to the other side of the world. The ships then following the unloading of all the European cargo, would then back load with Copra (coconut husks) bags of coffee beans, cocoa beans, and the tanks would be filled with hot vegetable oil which had to be kept at a certain temperature, otherwise it would solidify in the tanks, for the return trip to Europe.

The year before Donald had been offered the position of Purser. The company, in order to increase their revenue, decided upon the introduction of carrying passengers. So accommodation was altered, with swanky new double berth cabins being built for a total of eight passengers. A passenger lounge was also built for the exclusive use of passengers.

The cost for each passenger that would join the ship in Le Havre, and stay for the voyage of a lifetime was £8,000.00. However, it was a four month trip, and the ship would set sail from Europe, crossing the Atlantic to transit the Panama Canal, and then cruise the Pacific to Tahiti where the ship would stay for two days, before going on to Fiji, the Solomon Islands, French Caledonia, Vanuatu, Noumea, Papua New Guinea, New Zealand and Singapore. The ship would then return to Europe crossing the Indian Ocean and up through the Red Sea to the Suez canal, crossing the Mediterranean, sometimes calling at Cadiz. Then to Hull where the passengers would leave the vessel.

CHAPTER THIRTEEN
LIFE WITH BANK LINE

Donald had negotiated with the company that he would join the vessel at Le Havre, rather than the earlier port of Hull. Penny had undergone a hysterectomy operation, and whilst Donald was permitted to stay for an extra few days at home, the time frame was tight to join the FORTHBANK before the vessel sailed from Europe. Nanny Gwennie had agreed to stay with Penny, to help with convalescence and to look after the children.

Donald joined the ship in Le Havre, and met with the Purser who would be going home from that port. The crew consisted of British

Officers and a Bangladesh crew. Bank Line had employed Bangladesh ratings for years. They were hard working and friendly, and not only that, they were brilliant cooks, and the various curry dishes were famous all over the world, and especially with the company representatives and buyers dotted all over the South Pacific Islands, as when a Bank Line vessel visited these numerous ports, dignitaries and financial supporters of the company would be invited on-board and served sumptuous dinners. After all, who didn't like Curry, not the European versions, but made the way it should be, from the heart of Bangladesh.

Donald met with the Master, who had been with the company for years, and was an old hand of the Bank Line, a senior Captain. He met with the other senior officers, as Donald now was also a senior officer, as with the introduction of passengers and the revenue that passengers brought to the company, they required a senior officer to take care of their needs. After all, they were paying a premium cost, which in turn required a premium service. The Officers benefitted from the introduction of passengers, as the standard of shipboard catering had to be elevated to the expectations of the passengers, and passengers ate their meals with the officers in the dining saloon, so they all had the same standard of food.
The ratings on the other hand, their standard fare was curry based, they had their own separate galley to the main galley. They also had their own cook, who was called the Bhandari.

Donald then met the eight passengers. The off-signing Purser introduced Donald to the passengers who were sitting in their private lounge, an airy space that had been built on an upper deck, three sides panelled in glass offering panoramic views of the sea. There were an American couple, both elderly and retired called Bill & Elsie, then there was another American couple of similar age called Bob and Angela, and a lovely Finnish couple called Olly and Anna-Liese. Olly was in his sixties and Anna-Liese was a bubbly lady in her early fifties. She had been suffering with leukaemia, an intelligent woman who was a retired scientist. The last two passengers, were an old British couple called Derek and Clare. Derek was a bit of an old duffer, a little bombastic around the edges, but with a heart of gold. Clare was the long suffering wife, who was sweetness herself.

All the passengers were looking forward to the forthcoming adventure, and they were not treated like cattle on a regular cruise ship with hundreds of others. These people were important in their own right, whilst they were with the Bank Line. Donald was looking forward to this new challenge. He had a significant amount of experience with various people, and felt that he could weigh up a person's personality pretty quickly, and tune into their wave length ASAP.

During the fortnight that it would take to cross the Atlantic to the Panama Canal, Donald devised games and competitions that would keep the passengers amused. If a birthday was forthcoming, he would work in the galley and bake them a cake. He would make them birthday cards with caricatures of themselves on the front cover, this brought great amusement, as like everyone, people want to know how they are seen by other people. As he was reasonably proficient in the hair-cutting department, he would cut and trim the passengers' hair (even the ladies).

The weather improved as the ship travelled across the Atlantic, and it became warmer, and warmer, with endless sunshine on a daily basis. The vessel would transit the Panama Canal, and the passengers, by then, were pleased to be out on deck, looking through their binoculars at the land and canal, with the other ships at anchor waiting in a queue in readiness for transit. When it came for the vessel to go into the canal, the passengers were fascinated seeing the 'mechanical mules,' pulling the ship along through the various locks. The ship would then emerge on the other side of the canal and into the Pacific Ocean. Then there would be a long sea voyage down to Tahiti, which meant Donald had to find more distractions to keep the passengers from becoming bored. Donald was also responsible for the catering department, the bond and slopchest, laundry, accounts and all the other functions that he had undertaken when with previous companies. However, his main concern in this particular function, was the well-being of the passengers. It was imperative to the company that this source of revenue would be self-generating, and this could only be accomplished if the word spread that a trip with the Bank Line, was a must for everyone who could afford this trip of a life time, sailing around the world. Not many other cargo passenger ships were offering anything quite so glamorous, and for the period of four months.

Donald got along well with the Bangladesh crew, and became good friends with the Chief Cook. He was a terrific cook, who was hard working, intelligent and a great personality. He was a man of around 30 years, and married. He told Donald that he had married his wife when she was fourteen years old. Donald was a little shocked that anyone could be married at such a young age. Donald asked how the marriage was working out, as there was a big disparity between their ages. He said that all was fine. She would stay at home and do the cooking, and could only leave the house with a chaperone. So Donald asked if they got along well. The cook replied "Oh yes, but sometimes, she argues with me, and that is not good. But I give her a slap and she is fine!" Donald was astounded "You slap her?" He exclaimed. The cook, nodding sagely, and mimicking the movement with his hand replied "Yes, Slap, slap and all OK."

The cook and his wife had a young son who they called Sadam Hussein, named after the now dead Iraqi dictator. Sadam Hussein was the cook's hero. As it was coming up to the little boy's birthday. Donald made a large birthday card out of chart paper for the Cook to send to his little boy. It was Islam themed, and he was thrilled that Donald had taken the time to make this special card for his boy.

The open air swimming pool was situated on the upper aft deck of the ship. It was filled with sea water. Officers and passengers used to make use of the pool, though the ratings seemed to steer clear of the pool. As far as Donald was concerned, they had as much right to this facility as anyone else on-board.

He coerced the Chief Cook to accompany him to the pool, and though the Chief Cook was tentative, the Cook did accompany Donald, and he enjoyed a cool swim for an hour. There were remarks made by the officers after the event, but Donald was not fazed, and opposition to ratings using the pool would cause more embarrassment that it was worth.

When the ship reached Tahiti and the other South Pacific Islands, it was the responsibility of Donald to arrange the various shore going trips that entailed exploring the islands. There were picnics, speed boat rides, walks, historical sites, Japanese wartime relics from

World War Two. The best part of this responsibility was that Donald could accompany the passengers free of charge.

The passengers liked Donald, and Donald liked them.

One interesting country was Vanuatu. This country is a collection of islands that is south of the Solomon Islands and north of New Zealand. The island of Espiritu Santo was utilised by the US forces in World War Two to repel the Japanese from the Solomon Islands and the South Pacific. The Americans had invested millions of dollars in the infrastructure of the islands, and the Americans had imported thousands of tons of hardware, jeeps, trucks, munitions etc.

At the end of the conflict in 1945, the Americans offered the local government all the military hardware for a small nominal charge, as it would prove to be incredibly expensive to ship the hundreds of vehicles back to the United States. The local government thought that they would be canny and hold out for the Americans just to give them this fortune in hardware free of charge. They were sorely disappointed, as the Americans miffed at the greed of local government, decided not to give Vanuatu any of the equipment in working order, so all the hardware was driven into the sea, where it became useless to everyone. The site became known as 'million dollar point', and the rusting debris can still be seen there to this very day.

Another point of interest on the island of Espiritu Santo was a beautiful clear water lagoon that was situated in the middle of a forested glade. The water was pure and the colour of indigo, the most beautiful colour of water that Donald had set his eyes upon. The lagoon seemed bottomless, and Donald and the passengers enjoyed swimming in the pure clear cool waters. The lagoon had once been visited by the Hollywood actress Dorothy Lamoure who also appreciated the sheer beauty and tranquil setting. It became known soon after her visit, to be called 'The Dorothy Lamoure' Lagoon. Donald made a visit to the Lagoon twice a year, and he was always incredulous that the colour he tried to imprint in his mind faded, and was renewed upon each visit, the indigo colour was always more beautiful than he ever remembered.

The island of Espiritu Santo is noted for the raising of beef herd cattle. There was plenty of beef to export, but what they did lack was the import of lamb. Australian nationals, who wanted to get away from the humdrum of civilisation came to Vanuatu because it was set back in time, they came for the peace and wildness, which were both in abundance. They were not allowed to purchase properties of their own as in the 1970's a group of right wing American millionaires had tried to monopolise the country for their own playground. The government to ensure that this was never to be a threat to the country again, ruled that foreigners would never be able to own property or land, they could however rent property and businesses. So there were many ex pat Australians in Vanuatu, who either arrived on their own, or some brought their wives and children.

A lot of Australians liked eating lamb, and there was a shortage of this commodity, so when it did become available, it was well sought after.

The essence of this particular story was that Donald as Purser was informed of the glut of beef and the scarcity of lamb in Vanuatu, and that if Australians ever offered the Purser a deal, where they would supply the vessel with prime Santo fillet beef in exchange for lamb, kilo for kilo, that Donald must refuse, as customs were strict to this swap, and keen to put a stop to the trade. Donald was well aware that if he could swap, say 100kgs of prime fillet into the ships meat freezer locker at £9.50 per kilo, and part with 100kgs of Lamb Loins at £2.45 per kilo, he could be quid's in and it would boost the choice and quality on the menu, and improve his daily feeding costs.

He was approached by two Australians, who managed the Beef Santo Meat Packing Company, and they wished to proceed with this deal after dark. Donald thought what the Master had said in warning, but could not resist the lucrative temptation. After all it was a fair deal for the vessel, just an issue with the Customs and Excise. When the sun had gone down around 6pm one evening, Donald and his two new Australian pals, went below to the freezers, they had brought with them the four boxes of beef. The beef was stowed in the meat locker, and the Aussies picked up the four boxes of lamb loins. They were quietly bringing the boxes onto the open deck, when suddenly a customs truck appeared! The boxes were hurriedly dropped on the narrow deck outside the ships accommodation door, and the Aussies disappeared. By chance, the Captain came out onto the deck, and putting his foot on one of the bottom ships rail, he leaned out onto the upper rail with his elbows, to look out at the port. Donald was next to him, and although there was a box of lamb loins sitting on deck quite close to the Captain's feet. It was difficult to see how the Captain had not noticed the box. Donald thought that he had seen it, but that he had chosen to ignore it. The Captain, then said good night to Donald and stepped back into the accommodation. Donald waited another twenty minutes on deck, and the customs lorry eventually disappeared. The two Aussies came out of the darkness onto the dock and boarded the ship again. They quickly picked up the boxes of Lamb, and made a dash back down the gangway. Unfortunately, the customs had sprung a trap for them, and caught them red handed loading the boxes onto their truck. The Customs arrested them, and called to Donald that they would come on-board in the morning to talk to him. Donald now felt a sense of panic sweeping over him. Time in a prison in Vanuatu was not going to be a picnic that he would enjoy. However, God must have been smiling down sideways upon Donald, as later that night, a tropical storm picked up with enormous speed, and the vessel being unsafe at its mooring, was forced to let go, and the ship had to sail to a safe anchorage whilst the storm played itself out. The storm raged for two days before the ship returned back to port. By some unfathomable good fortune, the customs seemed to have 'forgotten the beef and lamb' incident, and this time, God was definitely on his side. Donald had got away with it. Phew!

Donald was missing his family very much on this his first trip with Bankline, and by Christmas the Ship would be making the journey home and would be calling at Singapore. The vessel had an approximate ETA at Singapore for around 21st December.
As Officers were entitled to bring their wives and family to sea at that time. Donald thought that this would be a good opportunity for his wife Penny and little Flick, to join the vessel at Singapore, for the journey across the Indian Ocean, though the Suez Canal and ultimately Rotterdam. Donald telephoned Penny with the suggestion, and at first, there was a lot to consider, as Belinda and Archie would be left behind at home, and was it fair just to take Flick? The children were considerate, and did not mind that their mother and sister would not be with them for Christmas. They liked Nanny Gwennie a lot, and knew that their Nanny would look after them. So, eventually, everyone agreed to the plan, and Penny and Flick made the flight from the UK to Singapore. It was a daunting

journey for Penny as she was not a seasoned traveller. It was also a huge responsibility caring for a small child, and travelling to the other side of the world. However, they arrived in Singapore safely, and the port agents met them at the airport, and drove them to the hotel. Flick had a cold, and was miserable, which did nothing to ease Penny's concerns. The next morning, they were taken to the pier, where they were helped board a launch, together with their suitcases. They made around a twenty minute trip from the port to the anchorage, where the vessel was stationed. Donald was waiting for them with eager anticipation on deck, and saw the approach of the launch, trying to catch a glimpse the images of his wife and child. The launch then came alongside the accommodation ladder, and Penny stepped gingerly from the launch as there was a heavy swell at the anchorage. She grabbed hold of the ships railing and climbed up the ladder to the ships deck, collapsing into Donald's arms weeping with exhaustion. Flick was being carried on-board by one of the crew of the launch, and Flick was happy to see her Daddy.

Donald carried Flick, and all three went into the accommodation and made their way to Donald's quarters. There was a Day room/office, a bedroom and en-suite bathroom. Penny unpacked whilst Donald entertained Flick. The Bangladesh crew, who loved children, made a fuss of Flick, and made any excuse to see her and to talk to her. She felt like a little celebrity. The officers and passengers were acquainted with Penny, and they all immediately liked her, as she had that innate ability to get along with everyone. They all loved her broad Somerset accent.

Penny and Flick spent their first couple of days settling into the ships routine. They sunned themselves on the open deck, swam in the swimming pool. Socialised in the officers' bar, where officers and wives cooed over Flick and made a fuss of her.

Christmas day arrived, and Donald was as usual, helping to arrange the Christmas lunch with the galley staff. Penny and Flick sat with the 3rd Engineer, Anna-Liese and Olly, and the young Irish 3rd Officer called Owen. They all enjoyed their lunch, and all officers and passengers ascended to the Officers bar for after dinner drinks. There was a dance party that evening, and a cold buffet had been set up for anyone who was still hungry. Penny enjoyed dancing with the passengers and Flick enjoyed dancing and singing and playing with her Christmas presents.

The next day on Boxing Day, after lunch Penny and Flick spent the afternoon in the Officers Bar watching television. Flick had the new release video of 'The Little Mermaid' as one of her Christmas presents, and she was allowed it to be shown on the TV in the bar. She sat watching it in total rapture, though she was not alone. Penny was amused, as she looked around the room to see that the Chief Engineer, and other Officers were equally enthralled with the little mermaid.

The ship carried on the journey, passing Sri Lanka then heading for the Red Sea and to the Suez Canal. Upon reaching the canal, shore-side boatmen boarded the vessel to assist in the transit. Whilst on-board, they also set up shop by selling souvenirs. There were so many souvenirs and trinkets that the aft deck looked more like an Egyptian Bazaar. Sailing out of the canal and across the Mediterranean the ship called at Cadiz, and although it was January, the weather was mild and Donald and family with Olly and Anna-Leise enjoyed an evening ashore in Cadiz.

The ship reached Rotterdam, the passengers left the vessel full satisfied with their round the world tour. The British Officers were also to leave the vessel and the relief Officers would replace them in Rotterdam. Donald, Penny and Flick left the ship at Rotterdam and boarded a plane home, and back to family life in Pudding Well, Somerset.

Donald was home on leave for around eight weeks, before he was assigned to the MV Clydebank, same type and class of ship as the Forthbank, but by this time, the company had decided to flag out their fleet of six vessels. This was due to taxation laws, in that it was in a shipping company's best interests from a financial point of view to place the responsibilities of crewing vessels to offshore contracts. This reduced employment costs, and so crewing companies sprang up in places all over the world from Singapore to the Cayman Island, Panama, Liberia and the Isle of Man and the Channel Islands. The Bank Line was now registered with the Isle of Man Ship Registry, and the previous registered port of London showing on the stern of all the vessels, was removed and replaced with Douglas, as this was the capital of the Isle of Man. Donald received a small redundancy package from the company and became employed by the crewing agency in the Isle of Man. It made no difference to Donald as to who he worked for, as it did not change the job description, or salary, and he carried on as before.

The Clydebank, now that the Bank Line had flagged out their vessel, started employing Polish and Filipino junior officers and making redundant some of the British junior officers. This did cause natural resentment, as humans by and large enjoy routine and resent change, although they can grumble that 'things never change!'

Some of the existing British officers yearned for the old days, when all the officers were British, and they didn't have to bother with having human cargo (passengers) on-board. By default, the Purser was also resented, and there was barely concealed hostility shown to the Purser and passengers.

The British Chief Officer was one who resented the new regime, and it was not long before he and Donald felt animosity between each other. Donald found him obnoxious and ignorant, but then again he had met many similar types over the years.

There was also a Scottish Electronic Engineer who resented the Purser and passengers. A skinny runt of a man, middle aged and cranky. He had ruddy facial features which became more florid, whenever he swigged back his usual copious daily amounts of Scotch whisky in the officers bar.

On one occasion, when Donald was conversing with two passengers in one of the public alleyways. The electrician, pushed rudely past Donald and muttered obscenities in his direction. The confrontation was unsettling and embarrassing for both Donald and the passengers. Donald glossed over the incident with his two passengers and left them.

He then followed the electrician, and cornered him in an alcove. Standing over the belligerent man in overalls, Donald put his face up to the Electrician's face and said "If you don't like me, that's fine with me. It doesn't bother me at all!" "You just keep out of my way, and I'll keep out of yours!" "Don't ever think of embarrassing me in front of my passengers again. Got it?"

The electrician seemed to have got the message. Donald would keep an eye on him.

The days passed seamlessly and all was well. One day as the breakfasts were being served to the officers and ratings in the Officers Saloon and crew messroom. There was another room for Officers in dirty boiler-suits for use to eat meals. The Scottish electrician ate his breakfast in this particular room which is called a 'Duty Mess'.

Donald heard hurried steps coming to his office, and the face of the Chief Engineer looked around Donald's open doorway and shouted "Hurry Don, you have to come to the Duty Mess, the electrician is choking!"

Donald hurried behind the Chief Engineer who was leading the way to the Duty Mess. Upon arrival, Donald saw that the electrician was standing up, gasping for breath, which was not reaching his lungs. It was obviously that the food had firmly lodged in his throat. The electrician, was now the colour of deep burgundy, and turning purple. Just for a nano second, a thought flitted through Donald's mind that retribution had been swift. Donald went behind the electrician, and grabbing him around the solar plexus, clutching his fists into the diaphragm, Donald gave a heaved inward and upward jerk, which caused, what was a rolled up ball of bacon, from the electrician's throat, to be ejaculated out of his mouth like an express train. The electrician, gulped in air with relief, and he quickly resumed his neutral florid features. He spluttered his thanks to Donald.

For the rest of the voyage, he remained courteous and polite whenever they crossed paths. The electrician appeared to have got over usual grouchy behaviour. Donald thought that he now appreciated his good fortune, in that not only was a Purser was on the ship, but also a person who was experienced with medical emergencies.

Four months on the CLYDEBANK were by and large enjoyed, as Donald had visited the similar ports and places on the well-trodden route that the Bank Line had taken for over a hundred years. The passengers were great fun and Donald had found that the position of being a Purser with passengers was definitely his niche. Whereas others sometimes found the role intimidating, Donald relished the experience, as he enjoyed meeting new people, and always liked to weigh his new passengers up in order that he could get the best out of them.

The trip went by and the passengers were enjoying the sights and the tours. Donald took them onto Champagne Beach in Vanuatu where the sand is white, and the views stunning. A picnic would be set up for the group and everyone could enjoy caviar and champagne. There was the opportunity to snorkel or even scuba dive, as the President Coolidge ship was sunk years before in the waters off Vanuatu, and scuba diving enthusiasts enjoyed investigating the sunken wreck.

The one unfortunate down side on the CLYDEBANK came when that Christmas and after serving the Christmas dinner to the Officers and passengers. The Captain, who was the same Master that Donald had sailed with on the PALACIO as a Cook/Steward, and who had recommended Donald for the post of Purser, sent a message via a deck officer for Donald to some to see him in his cabin.

The news was that Donald's mother, Margo had passed away on Christmas Eve. She had been sat in her usually chair. Walter was sleeping in another chair. The 6pm news was about to start. Walter had woken up and talked to Margo, as she was quiet and still. He got up and touched her to find that she had passed away.

Donald was upset to hear that his mother had died. He had only the year before taken both His mother and father by car to Glasgow for a week's holiday where Margo was admitted into a nursing home during their stay. Walter had stayed at the nursing home with Margo, while Donald and his dog Lady, stayed at a B & B nearby. When Walter had initially asked Margo if she would like to go to the city of her birth with him. She refused point blank, but when Donald said that he would take them, she was in full agreement.

Now she was gone. Donald had last spoken to his mother when the CLYDEBANK was in Lae, Papua New Guinea. She had talked to Donald but at that time had a heavy cold. Donald now wished he had contacted her again, but he was not to know that she was so close to death.

He was unable to be repatriated, as the vessel was still calling at ports in Papua New Guinea, and there was nothing that could be done during the Festive Season with limited flights and travel. So he was unable to attend his mother's funeral in early January. Penny had to represent him at the Church.

Although the life at sea always suited Donald. Now that he had a family, he was more and more wanting to be settled ashore so that he could be home with Penny and the children and see them growing up. As Donald was an animal lover, he considered that if he could find a job working with animals, then he would have a job that would be equally as fulfilling as the role of Purser.

Donald applied to become an RSPCA Inspector whilst he was still on-board another vessel. During his leave from that vessel, and whilst continuing his application, he worked free of charge at a local quarantine kennels in Ilminster. This was before pet passports were available, and there were no vaccines available for pets to protect them from contracting rabies.

Donald enjoyed mucking out the kennels, and being amongst the many friendly dogs who wagged their tails on his arrival, jumping up at him, and giving out great larruping sloppy licks. There was a little Dachshund dog in the kennels. She was unfortunate, as her owners who were part of the British army and had been stationed in Germany, brought the dog back with them. However, they had run out of funds, and could not afford to pay the fee at the end of the six month quarantine. So Tiika, the dachshund had been cooped up in the kennel for nine months, and she was beginning to feel the mental strain of incarceration. She took to Donald straightaway, and jumped up excitedly whenever she saw him. He in turn, loved the dog, and did his best to stay with her in her kennel for longer and longer periods, in order to keep her company. Tiika did not like the boss of the quarantine kennels, and he could never get near her. Whenever he approached her kennel, she would snarl and bark at him frantically. Donald asked his boss, as Tiika had passed her scheduled time in quarantine, whether he could walk the dog during his lunch period. The boss was apprehensive, agreeing, though warned him that the dog should not escape, as the owners may want her back at some point. Donald said that he would ensure that she would be fine, and from then on he let Tiika run free on the many walks in the Forest. She was so pleased to enjoy freedom at last that her mental condition improved. On a walk, she never moved far from Donald. She would stand by him loyally. The fact is that they were both obsessed with each other. Eventually the owners agreed a financial deal with the kennels and collected Tiika. Donald never forgot her.

CHAPTER FOURTEEN
STUDENT INSPECTOR

The RSPCA usually accepted two classes a year for the eight month course as a student inspector. However, in 1991 when Donald applied for a position in the class. There would only be one class that particular year. Around two and a half thousand people apply for the training course, and there were only twelve places available in 1992. The RSPCA were aware that Donald had been working free of charge at a quarantine kennel, and Donald was unsure that this is what swayed the RSPCA to accept him for the enrolment in the class. Upon his written acceptance. Donald resigned as Purser with the Bank Line.

The RSPCA course takes place at the RSPCA headquarters in Horsham, West Sussex. Eight months training is required due to the extensive learning to be undertaken, ensuring that as an Inspector, the individual is fully versed in the knowledge, and the legislation involving animal welfare.

At 40 years old, Donald was the oldest in the class. The eleven other lucky applicants included a paramedic, an ex-army sergeant, an ex-police constable, a Hong Kong Police Inspector, a Science teacher, an equestrian, a beauty therapist, just to name a few.

Donald travelled by car to Horsham, and the RSPCA had organised accommodation for each student inspector. Everyone stayed at private homes as lodgers with the resident owners. Donald was accepted into a home run by an elderly lady who was a widow, and she provided Donald with excellent meals.

For the first six weeks, there would be a five day week of classes held in the training room at the Headquarters, which was a grand spacious old building with its own grounds in Horsham town centre. It used to be a Grammar School. The headquarters were lavish and very well equipped. Donald and the other students were kitted out with full uniform and working clothes. The cost of the course in those days cost around £13,000 per student, so it was an extremely costly business to train Inspectors.

Training was strict and regimental. It was just like being back in the sea school. Lots of standing to attention and marching. Getting up when anyone senior entered the room. It certainly wasn't a place for fun and frivolity! That was a pity, as Donald was born with a whacky out of sync personality, and would find that trying to stay serious for eight months would be virtually impossible and also unbearable. You have to get the laughs in life as often as you can.

Donald had brought one of the early word processors with him. It was a step up from an electric typewriter, and would enable him to type up a lot of his work neatly. However, he made use of it in the run up to the first of the exams, at the end of the first six week period. Together as a class, questions that may come up in the exam period, together with the answers were typed up on the word processor, and each student would swot up on the information.

They had during classwork had to write an essay on a scenario where an Inspector was called to a house to investigate a report of cruelty to a dog. While the other students wrote sombre essays explaining in detail the RSPCA procedures. Donald took another tack, where the owner was a Swedish Masseuse, who offered her services to Donald, instead of acknowledging any cruelty to her animal. Donald felt that the story was at least imaginative, whilst capturing the essence of a home visit, in animal welfare terms. Unfortunately the course tutors thought otherwise, considering Donald to be a wide boy, who was set on belittling their learning programme. It was nothing further from the truth, as Donald could knuckle down to hard work, but felt that it did not all have to be dull and boring, a little humour would do no harm. This put Donald on track as class target. He had been a target before, though little did he know that they don't forgive a misdemeanour lightly in the RSPCA.

Donald passed the first set of exams. There were then courses held at agricultural colleges with lodgings and also a week at the Animal Hospital Harmsworth in London. There was also a course held at an abattoir, and this was one course that Donald did not like at all. The experience of attending an abattoir, when frightened cattle were herded in, and the smell of blood was thick in the air. Each student had to perform euthanasia with the aid of a captive bolt, which is a pistol, with an explosive charge that fires a bolt out of the barrel at a speed of 500 miles per hour, into the brain of the animal. It was a horrible experience, and left Donald traumatised for some time.

There was a course on a farm, which involved removing horns from sheep and castrating pigs. There was a course with a farrier where each student would remove a horse shoe from one of the many amputated legs of dead horses. The whole experience was very different to what Donald had been used to but he did as he was told, and learned quickly as he wanted to be a good inspector.

The eleven other students were pleased that Donald had taken up the mantle to be the class joker, this would mean that there was less pressure on them to be exposed to criticism and negativity as course tutors would already have their work cut out with Donald.

Whenever, Donald had to take his turn to stand in front of the class and speak on a subject that had been allocated to him. Donald would slowly raise himself from his chair, and with deliberate motions, make his way to the front of the class. He was well aware that his movements were already causing a stir in class, and his classmates were warming up in expectation, and already beginning to chuckle as to how his talk would proceed. They were never disappointed. As Donald began the first sentence of his talk, his audience would erupt with laughter. It was as if they had their favourite comedian on stage, and whether or not you heard the joke, it didn't matter, because you expected that it was going to be funny anyway. The uncontrolled laughter used to make the visiting lecturer, who had not previously met Douglas, sit up and look around with a look of consternation, as to why the class were laughing and acting out of character.

Sometimes the laughter could be heard in the adjoining classroom, and induce the course instructor to open the classroom door, look in, and see who was the cause of such merriment. He would shake his head, and say "I might have known and then leave the room.

The theory concerning animal welfare took place predominantly at the Horsham headquarters. There were two field training posts that were included in the eight month course programme. The field training involved student inspectors being dispatched to two groups that could be anywhere in England or Wales. One of the field stations is usually a group where the student resides, so that he or she could stay at home with their family whilst working with the group. The other station would be far from their homes, and they would be accommodated with one of the resident inspectors in that particular group.

For Donald, when the assignments were announced. He found that he was the only student inspector not to be given a home field station, so he would not have the comfort of being home with his family for both six week assignments. This is the time that Donald began to suspect that the organisation was looking for him to dislodge himself from the course. For all previous training courses, there had always been at least one casualty that never made the grade, and left the course without qualifying. This would suit any organisation, as dropping out of a course encourages the remaining students to behave and do well, and also do as they were told.

Although he understood the situation quite clearly, as he understood well enough the psyche of the human mind. He realised that he had to do what he had done all of his life. Knuckle down and stick like s**t to a blanket. His stubbornness would surprise his instructors.

The first field training went quickly enough, and he lodged with a fully qualified inspector. He learned a lot, and did as he was told, and just got on with his work. So when the six week assignment came to an end, Donald was handed an envelope with his appraisal by the Chief Inspector, and this was to be handed to the Chief Inspector in the group of his second, six seek assignment which happened to be in West Yorkshire. As Donald always held a natural suspicion of others, he was intrigued as to what the appraisal revealed. So, in his room that evening, he steamed open the envelope. He was intrigued to read that the advice from one chief inspector to the other was 'Work him as hard as you can, and do not allow him anytime off!' Donald resealed the envelope, and his suspicions were well founded. He was indeed the selected student that was to be expunged at any cost. Donald's resolve stiffened. He had left a decent job at sea to become an Inspector. And he was not a quitter. He would leave when he wanted to, and not when his employers wanted him to.

Donald survived his second field training assignment, and they were true to their word. He was run ragged for six weeks. He returned to headquarters in Horsham, he completed the full eight months, passing all the final exams, and for the first time, a full class, had graduated with all students.

Donald was given the extra pip on his epaulettes. A police check had been carried out, and Donald was issued with a licence to carry firearms. He was issued with a single shot pistol and bullets, a captive bolt, with a pack of explosive charges, and a first aid box with the appropriate drugs. He was also issued with a second hand Ford Escort van.

He was assigned to the Group One covering the West Midlands and Staffordshire, which was a part of Region 6.

CHAPTER FIFTEEN
QUALIFIED INSPECTOR

The Drinkwaters would have to move house from Somerset to Staffordshire. This meant that the children would have to change schools, so there would be big changes and an upheaval, before life could return to normal. The RSPCA funded a one bed maisonette for Donald on a large housing estate in the village of Perton. This was a short term accommodation agreement, until the family's home was sold, and they could purchase their own property.

A detached property was eventually purchased in the small village of Bishops Wood, which is just off the A5 between the town of Stafford and Telford. Archie would attend the middle school at Brewood, and Belinda would go to the High School at Penkridge. Flick would go to the little primary school a five minute walk from home in Bishops Wood.

The children settled in very quickly and Belinda was soon talking in a Black Country accent. It is surprising how quickly a brain can adapt in order for a person to fit quickly into a new community.

When Donald was assigned to his new posting. He was unsure if it was a decent allocation, where there would be lots of facilities and enough funds to back up Inspectors, who would have to collect sick and injured animals, and their treatment would require funding. As he was not exactly the teacher's pet when he was at the training school, he did not think that he would be given special treatment. He was not wrong there. The Staffordshire group had very limited funds with limited resources, so another challenge awaited Donald in his new career.

He met with his fellow colleagues in Group 1. Sandra was the Chief Inspector, then there were another five inspectors who would work with Donald. There was Kelvin who covered Burton upon Trent, where there was an animal home. Then there was Dolly and John who covered Stoke on Trent, then Nigel who covered Stafford town, and last but not least there was Deborah who covered the posh part of Wolverhampton, whilst Donald was left with the poorer end.

Group one, was indeed a very busy group. Lots of issues with travellers' camps and neglected horses, animal cruelty in Wolverhampton, and road traffic accidents involving dogs and cats. There was an on call system, where Inspectors' would take weekly turns in looking after the entire county on their own following the end of a day shift on every week day, and then on call throughout the weekend. Being on call was both gruelling and tiring. A call would be received to go to Stoke on Trent to rescue an animal, and then another call again to return to Wolverhampton for another a rescue, animal cruelty complaint, then a third call to travel to Burton upon Trent, then further calls for Wolverhampton, Stoke or indeed any town or village in the County. So an Inspector would criss-cross the county over and over, for hours on end. There were times when an Inspector could be busy for up to fifteen hours at a time.

There were many rescues, for instance, Donald was called to a house where a sparrow had somehow trapped itself between the two layers of plaster and brickwork in the kitchen of someone's home. Donald would hack a hole in the wall, and then retrieve the little bird. Unfortunately, there was a large ugly hole in the kitchen which he had to leave behind.

Another case involved a cat wedged between two walls, and Donald had to hack chunks out of the wall, and using washing up liquid, reach into the cavity and gently slide the cat out.

He was called by the Police to a junction on the M6, where a swan had landed on the central reservation, thinking that it was landing on a stretch of water. The Police had stopped the traffic on both sides of the motorway, and it was at a complete standstill. Motorists enjoyed the spectacle of Donald chasing the swan down the central reservation with a swan hook, and then rugby tackling the swan into submission, before wrapping it in a canvas bag, taking it away and relocating it.

Donald was called to rescue of a cat stranded high up in a tree in Wolverhampton. In order to save calling the Fire Brigade, Donald saw a refuse lorry approaching, so he asked the driver if he would stop his lorry by the tree. Donald scrambled onto the roof and with an extendable noose, he caught the cat and brought it down to safety, though he nearly fell off the roof himself in the process.

There was a call to rescue a bull who had its head stuck in a metal feeder in the middle of a field. It was a fully-fledged bull that did not look too happy in its predicament. Donald brought the hack saw out of the van and sitting on the feeding trough, he sawed through one of the bars, and once the bar was sawn through, he bent the bar back sufficiently, for the bull to extract his horns out the trough. Donald then ran like the clappers across the field, and leapt over the fence.

There were times when an inspector could be called for collection of birds and animals that ended up as a complete waste of time. The public were always well meaning, but sometimes it would have been quicker if they had taken an injured bird or animal to a local vet, rather than call the RSPCA for an inspector who was many miles away. Donald was called to a house in Wolverhampton for a sparrow. When he arrived at the house, a lady opened the door holding a little box not much bigger than a matchbox, and there was a little sparrow lying on a bed of cotton wool. Unfortunately the bird was dead, and rigor mortice was well and truly advanced. Donald thanked the lady and took the bird away for disposal.

Once when a trainee inspector was travelling with Donald one of the busy weekend callouts. The phone rang, and a call came in to travel from Wolverhampton to McDonald's in Stoke on Trent to pick up an injured pigeon. Upon arrival in Stoke on Trent, and saying to Kim, the trainee Inspector "Watch this Kim!" She followed Donald, who had picked up a cardboard carrier, and they entered the McDonald's, striding up to the counter. A girl behind the counter came up to the pair, and Donald, thrusting the cardboard carrier onto the counter said 'I'll have a pigeon mc nuggets please, to take out!" The girl looked back at him in mute silence, she then gathered her thoughts and led him and Kim outside to the rear of the shop and pointed to the sick pigeon lying in a box. Donald stooped down, and took the pigeon out of the box. It was immediately apparent, that the pigeon was dead. It was cold, and as stiff as a board. Donald looked at the girl saying "This pigeon is no more, it is deceased, and it will never fly again!" Donald popped the pigeon back in the box, chuckling as he did so. The girl, who thought that there should be at least a small service, followed by a wake, was not amused.

Once when a young local man expressed an interest in joining the RSPCA. He was assigned to shadow Donald for some work experience, and to see if he could see himself as an Inspector one day. Donald had previously been to see a horse belonging to a gypsy traveller, and had given a warning to the owner to improve on the care of the animal. So Donald was now returning to see if his advice had been heeded. The day was cold, and it had started to snow, with a cold wind whipping across the field, as Donald and his work experience friend, traipsed to where the horse was grazing. All of a sudden, a man mountain appeared over the ridge, striding forcefully toward the pair. It could be seen that he meant business, he happened to be the son of the man Donald had berated a few days earlier. As he approached, Donald's mobile phone rang, and Betty, one of the dispatchers came onto the line. The man mountain came at Donald with fists flailing, shouting and swearing abuse at Donald. Who then put up his hand as a sign of peace, speaking into the voice piece of his phone "Can't talk now Betty, I am just heading for a punch-up, and will be rolling around for a while, in the middle of a field!" The aggressive muscleman had listened to this interaction, and when Donald looked calmly at him, he instantly deflated, and allowed Donald to tell him that he was not here to harass his father, but only to check on the condition of the horse. The man muttered and growled, and then did an about turn and disappeared over the brow of the hill. Donald looked toward his young protégé, and he was shocked to see that the poor lad was ashen, white and shaking. By the time he had got over the tremors, he informed Donald that this was not the job for him, thanks very much. He did not need the aggro!

Donald was involved with quite a few crazy members of the public from time to time. He was called to a house where it was reported that a husband and wife were being cruel to two young puppy dogs. When Donald called at the house, there was a balding man in a string vest and underpants slapping white emulsion paint onto the walls. His wife also had a brush in her hand and was slapping paint on in the same manner. Music was blaring out. They did indeed looked to be quite mad as they were shouting and rambling and being totally incoherent. Donald looked into the front room and saw to young puppies shivering and cowering under the table. It could be seen that they were both petrified. Donald checked them, and they were well fed, and disappointingly, Donald could not take them away. There was no proof of neglect, and it was not a crime for lunatics to own animals.

Donald attended court on many occasions as the prosecuting officer, and had to give evidence. Inspectors were responsible for building case files, taking photographs for evidence, and taking statements from the offenders and any witnesses. The procedure was strict and the file had to be totally accurate in order to present a case in the magistrates' court.

When Donald was building a case, he would undertake contemporaneous interviews. All inspectors used long hand, by writing the questions and answers, and then asking the interviewee to read the statement fully and then initial each answer and finally sign the statement. The statement would then be typed up for presentation to the Legal Superintendents' at Horsham. Donald considered that it was unfair to the person being interviewed to have to read someone else's writing which could sometimes be difficult to read. So he bought a portable type writer, which he would use whilst conducting an interview. It was easy for the person to read, and there was also the advantage that the Inspector would not have to type out the contemporaneous interview for headquarters. It was killing two birds with one stone. The legal superintendents' had never seen anything like it and they did not like change in any form. They tried to stop Donald's initiative by saying that if he lost the type writer then they would not be obliged to buy him a new one. Donald assured them that he would never ask them to fund another machine, and that he would replace a lost type writer at his own cost. They backed down, and had to accept that Donald's initiative did after all make sense, and it was fairer to the interviewee.

There were insufficient resources, which made life incredibly difficult when animals required collection, but there was nowhere to take them. The local branch baulked at the veterinary bills that were accrued, as they had limited funds. Donald was forever taking animals and birds home with him. He had bought an outside concrete kennel with a small wired run, and placed it in his back garden. There were seven dogs at his home on one occasion, and the neighbours' kicked up a fuss, when all the dogs started barking together, all at the same time. Donald couldn't blame them. Sometimes he had a mix of ducks with ducklings, cats, dogs, pigeons and ferrets. The house was looking more like a menagerie on a daily basis.

Donald had to euthanize various birds and animals, and each occasion left a scar with Donald. He realised that he could not save all the birds and animals, but he didn't like killing them either.

He went to rescue a sick sheep once, stranded in woodland and it was a dark night. He located the sheep, but it had already died. He wanted to retrieve the body rather than let it rot in the wood, and was hauling it up over a style, when the sheep lolled its head into Douglas' face. Anyone seeing this image would think that Donald and the sheep were smooching, or even practicing for a strictly come dancing debut!

Donald enjoyed a lot of TV, Radio and newspaper fame for his case files, and he never failed to ensure that the media were available for a high profile RSPCA case. He also enjoyed giving talks on animal welfare to children at the Wolverhampton's schools. He would have regular slots at various schools, and teachers appreciated the time Donald took to come and help children, some who were deprived, and in unhappy homes. They were great kids, and Donald hoped that most would escape the poverty trap, and the violence, that they suffered in their own homes.

As Donald's case file was high amongst Inspectors. There was one week that he won the 'Inspector of the Week Award' which meant best inspector throughout the force. Donald was bemused that he had received this title, as he believed that if the people who had selected him knew him, they would have thought twice about it, and would have offered it to somebody else.

After nearly five exhausting years with the RSPCA, Donald needed a rest, and thought it was time to pack it in, so he tendered his resignation, and travelled to Horsham to return all his kit, together with his vehicle. One of the administrative officers performed a leaving interview, and with a concerned look and glum expression, he informed Donald that he was sorry to see him go. Donald had heard similar twaddle many times before, and said to the officer "You don't even know me!" "Let's forget the insincere flattery and not waste time!"
Donald left the building, and a great weight was lifted from his shoulders. The experience in the Society was tremendous, but he did not want to grow old in the RSPCA.

The best part of being shore-side was being at home with Penny and the children. Donald always took an active interest in their schooling. As he had not done so well with schooling as a child, he tried to make up for the lack of education by living through the children's homework. Belinda accepted very little help. She was a girl that had to do the work herself, as if she had to try and prove something. Not that she had anything to prove as she was a naturally brilliantly academic and had nothing to prove.

Archie was also a bright boy, though like many other boys, he preferred to focus on his computer games, and his scalextric. So it was easy for Donald to look at either his English, Art and History homework, and take over. Donald was always pleased when Archie told him that his homework had gone down a storm.
Flick was also getting good reports from the head teacher at the primary school, so Donald was really pleased that he had three really clever children with such a great future ahead of them. He always encouraged them to do well, and to learn as much as possible, and attain the best grades and hopefully go to University.
When Archie was eleven, Donald wanted him to attempt to gain a scholarship to go to a private boys' school. Archie was lukewarm about the idea, as he was happy in his current school with all of his friends. Donald persevered, and in an attempt to win Archie over, he promised him a brand new bicycle, if he went on the scholarship

course. Donald bought him the new cycle, and was disappointed that Archie had changed his mind about the scholarship. However, Archie had a change of heart again when he was thirteen, and went for the scholarship, and he passed with flying colours. He was accepted into Adams Grammar School for boys. Donald was pleased beyond relief. It was not snobbery, but in reality he just wanted Archie to do well, and achieve where he did not.

When Archie went to the Grammar School, Donald used to 'bull' his school shoes up for him, until they shone like glass. Unfortunately, the other boys in his year, noticed the shininess, and would tread dirt from their shoes into Archie's. This did not deter Donald, as by the next morning, they would be gleaming again ready for Archie.

CHAPTER SIXTEEN
TRIP OF A LIFETIME

Upon resigning as an RSPCA Inspector. Donald was exhausted after nearly five years, where there had been many times of stress involved with the work. So he was looking forward to work which guaranteed more enjoyment without the stress. Donald contacted the Personnel Manager from his previous employer the Bank Line. The manager was pleased to hear from Donald, and informed him that there was a vacancy for a Purser, and as Donald was still well thought of even after nearly five years away from the company. He was offered the position of Purser. The company was very generous as they insisted on paying Donald the top rate of pay without losing his seniority in rank. This was indeed generous, and Donald was happy to accept the position.

A lot had changed in nearly five years. The company's old fleet had been scrapped due to the age of the ships. The company had to source replacement vessels that had to be the correct class, and size in order to be of sufficient draft, to gain access to the home port of Hull. Also giving thought to all the other small ports in the various South Pacific Islands. The ships had to be roll on-roll of vessels, allowing access of motor vehicles. They required sufficient deck space for containers, and of course, they required tanks, and all the complicated pipe work, and heating system in order to carry vegetable oil successfully. There was no glut of these types of vessels available in the shipping market. However, with the fall of the Soviet Union, and the creation of the Republic of Russia, six ice class vessels became available from the ex-Soviet Merchant Fleet. They were previously commissioned to transport goods to the northern ports of the Soviet Union, and these ports experienced frozen seas during the long winter months, so access to the ports required vessels with thick hulls that would be able to break the ice and allow access to the frozen ports. These ships were the right size and tonnage for the Bank Line, but they required modification in constructing the oil tanks and associated pipework, pumping station and heating coils. The company purchased the six vessels for ten million pounds each.

In dry-dock, the vessels were modified, and twelve luxury cabins, together with a residents lounge was renovated for the use of passengers.

Another change from the old days was a complete change with crewing nationalities. The Master, Chief Officer, Chief Engineer and Purser remained British. Though at times, The Chief Officer was sometimes a Russian national. All the other Officers were Russian, and all of the ratings were also Russian, who were employed from an agency in Vladivostok. This time, ratings were not exclusively male. There was a female second cook & baker, and four stewardesses. The only male catering rating was the Chief Cook.

Donald joined the MV FOYLEBANK at the George V dock in the port of Hull. He met with the Purser that was being repatriated in Hull. Donald met with the Master, Officers and crew, and familiarised himself with the vessel and his role as Purser. The ship sailed from Hull and to Le Havre where she was to load the last of the cargo before crossing the Atlantic Ocean to the Panama Canal.

When the ship arrived at Le Havre. Donald made preparations to receive the arrival of the twelve passengers.

A cocktail party had been arranged as a reception for them, and to be held in the Officers bar. Donald stepped ashore onto the dock, when he saw the coach roll up alongside the vessel. He had descended the accommodation ladder, and waited for them to alight from the bus. He introduced himself and shook hands with them all, and allowing the crew to organise bringing their baggage on-board. Donald led them up the accommodation ladder to their quarters. They showed great appreciation and were pleasantly surprised with their spacious en-suite cabins. Donald left them to settle in, and informed them that a reception party had been arranged for them in two hours at the Officers Bar.

They all trooped into the bar at the scheduled time, and Captain John Millar and senior officers made each passenger welcome. Donald looked at the contingent of people that he would be responsible for over a period of four months. The challenge was for him to ensure that each passenger enjoyed the trip, and would tell their friends, who would in turn, would generate new business for the Bank Line.

There was a Chinese lady, who was a single traveller. She was of slight build with short cropped blond hair, wearing vivid red lipstick on pursed lips. She stood sideways on nodding and talking to the Captain, holding her wine glass by the base of them stem between finger and thumb.

There was another passenger, a man in around his later fifties. He had swept back white hair. He stood with an expansive air, and was wearing a white shirt, double breasted suit jacket and trousers, and shiny leather shoes. He had a broad East End of London accent.

Then there were two Frenchmen, Jacque & Bernie, who were taking a break from their wives. They were both in their seventies, their English was brilliant, though obviously heavily accented.

There was an American couple, Louise and her husband Harry. Louise was a large lady in her eighties. She may have been old and heavy, but she had plenty of spirit, and she was loud! Her husband was wizened and skinny, a quiet and unassuming man, though Donald would have thought that he did not have a lot of choice as Louise made enough volume for both of them. Another American couple was Earl and Barbara. They were an elderly couple from New York, who were pleasant and well presented. Last but not least, there was Ken & Jean Humble, a British couple who lived in London.

This was a typical mix of passengers, though by and large, they were mostly in the older age group, as they were retired and had more opportunity to take four months away at sea, against younger people still in employment.

Over the next few days, Donald familiarised himself with his passengers. He warmed to them as individuals, and they warmed to him. Because Donald enjoyed his work, this came across in his persona as he ensured that each passenger was made to be the most important person in the world. These people had paid a lot of money to sail on old cargo ships tramping over the world. So they deserved the best that was available.

Donald went into the passenger lounge during one of those early days, and there was only one passenger in the room. Sitting back in an armchair and scrolling through a magazine. It was the gentleman with the swept back white hair, the man with the east end accent and the gangster suit he had seen at the reception. He was now wearing an open necked short sleeved shirt, shorts and flip flops.
Douglas asked if he could sit with him, and the gentleman agreed. It was the start of a tremendous relationship between the two men. The passenger's name was Raymond Pierrepoint, Ray, to his friends. Donald was to learn that he was distantly related to the past hangmen of the Pierrepoint family. The following is a brief glimpse of Ray, his upbringing and his ultimate success.
Ray was born in the east end of London in 1939. He was from a poor family, who struggled to make ends meet. Ray attended school but did not leave with any academic qualifications as he opted out of school at the age of fourteen. He was a born entrepreneur. He started by selling potatoes from an old pram in the east end streets. When he was seventeen, he was a runner for the notorious Richardson Gang, who were the adversaries of the Kray twins. Ray battled the daily struggle of survival during the 1950's and 60's. He had a nose for business and retailed reconditioned industrial equipment to catering establishments'. His businesses grew and his outlets and income grew at great speed. He became a millionaire. He moved to Sheerness in Kent, where he lived with his wife Bernice and two young sons. Ray became a mason, and in time was the Grand Wizard of the Lodge. Throughout all of his struggles and hardship, and his ascendency to ultimate wealth and privilege, Ray never forgot his roots. He never lost his perspective of being working class, and held no delusions of grandeur. Although he had become an assured and confident man, he was also remained humble.

Donald knew, after getting to know Ray, he had indeed found a very special person, so very different from the norm. Donald could admire the personality, coupled with the obvious grit that this man possessed, making this man a giant amongst men.

Ray was travelling on his own, as his wife did not think she would like to be away from her children, and grandchildren for a period of four months. Ray was a seasoned traveller, and had sailed on other passenger cargo vessels, so he had seen a lot of the world. He was a generous man, and although he liked the company of the Captain and senior officers, they warmed to him, as much as he warmed to them. On arrival at Tahiti, Ray invited Donald and the Captain ashore for a swanky meal at an expensive Chinese Restaurant. He would not hear of any help in paying the bill, he just enjoyed his own generosity. It was not before long that Ray, Donald, the Captain and others would troop ashore together at various tropical ports. Donald would have to admit that he did show more bias toward Ray than the other passengers, though he did still treat the other passengers well, but just not as well as he did with Ray.

Donald used to write a fortnightly newsletter for the ship which was available to the Officers, ratings and passengers. Donald would keep an eye on everything that was going on, and if there was a story that he could he could enlarge upon and make it funny, then the story would feature in the newsletter, together with caricatures. In one newsletter, Ray was the main brunt of the story, which depicted him in an unflattering manner (which did not bother Ray at all). However Donald had likened Ray to Saint Francis of Assisi. (The following is the transcript that Donald put into print for the ships newspaper)

ACCOLADES FOR RAYMOND

During the past three months on Foylebank, Mr Raymond Pierrepoint has without fear of contraception endeavoured to provide a focal fun point on-board. And his achievements have not gone unnoticed. Today, he receives from his fellow passengers, generous thanks for providing the group with originality, pots of fun and a genuine care for his fellow man. The spokesman for the group, Professor Bernie Aubert said yesterday "Ray is a great fellow, and we are all grateful to him for providing us with his warmth and great sense of humour & wit. He has certainly been a great input into our small select group." With regard to this tribute, Professor has wrote a small verse in appreciation:

Somewhere in what is now called Sheerness, quite a while ago. A boy was born from a poor family. He was the kindest sort towards men and animals, which he considered as his brothers. He worked hard, and became a man of means. However, one day. He decided to give up all his wealth and treasures, and put on a brown robe and sandals, and went away to 'relieve' others misfortunes. His name was RAYMOND, and he came from London. This is his prayer to His Creator:

"LORD, make me an instrument of Thy Peace
Where there is hatred, let me sow Love
Where there is injury, let me sow Pardon
Where there is doubt, let me sow Faith
Where there is despair, let me sow Light
And where there is sadness, let me sow Joy
GRANT that I may not so much seek to be consoled
As to console;
To be understood, as to understand
To be loved, as to Love
For it is in giving, that we receive; and it is
In pardoning that we are pardoned

The story was a hit with the officers and crew, and also appreciated by Ray. But there was uproar from some of the other passengers, with the main opposition coming from the Chinese lady passenger, who Donald had come to call 'China Lil' (but not to her face). China Lil had taken umbrage that Ray should be associated with such a revered figure as Saint as Francis of Assisi, and thought that Donald was being sacrilegious. Donald had to pacify her, and tell her that the newsletter was not meant to be taken seriously, and all was meant in good humour. Her ruffled feathers soon flattened out, and she calmed herself down. China Lil was the exact opposite of Ray. She was brought up with money and privilege, spoilt and shallow, with not a lot of thought for other people, as she was too concerned, and wrapped up in her own well-being.

Figure 12   The Drinkwater Family

Figure 13 MV Texaco Westminster

McLENINS IN ST PETERSBURG
Report by Freddie

A new chain of fast food takeaways have emerged in Russia called *Mc Lenins*. This is an exciting new venture in the East, and it is hoped that the idea will catch on to the ordinary folk on the street. Similar to *McDonalds* in the West, but with many subtle differences in the menu. To start with there is to be launched a special delicacy called...........''Pigeon McNuggets!'' This dish is going to be a real winner, and by luck my very good friend and General Manager of *McLenins* Mr Yuri Andropov Breshnev has given me the recipe. Here goes.........

Take one very young baby Racing Pigeon, marinade for six long hours in a pint of VB or Fosters Beer, remove and towel dry, sprinkle liberally with Drambuie and Baileys Irish Cream Liquor, cradle and mould the pigeon into a round comfortable shape, stroking down any ruffled young feathers, and bake in a short crust pastry for 20 minutes in a moderate oven until crispy brown and crackling! Serve in a basket with a pickled egg.

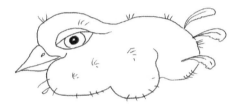

Pigeon McNugget

Figure 14 Excerpt from Ship's News Letter - Ray's Snail/Pigeon

Figure 15   Bank Line   MV Arunbank

Figure 16 RSPCA Inspector Donald Drinkwater

Figure 17 Self Portrait Of Donald

China Lil never took to the two old French gentlemen passengers. Even though they were educated and professional gentlemen, where Jacque was a linguist, and could speak a dozen languages. They did their best not to offend China Lil, in order that they could just enjoy their holiday without any unnecessary conflict. However, one day, there was an issue with the ship's sanitary plant, and the aroma of human sewage wafted into China Lil's cabin. China Lil was on the rampage and summoning the Chief Officer and other senior officer to her cabin, to get a whiff of the offending odour. She announced that she knew who the culprits where! She announced, saying loudly to the group "It's those Frenchies! I know it is! I can smell the garlic!"   Of course, the allegation was completely ludicrous, and everyone thought that China Lil was totally off her head.

She was nobody's favourite as she was as false as a cartload of monkey's and just moaned about everything and anything. However, Donald put up with her tantrums, as he was the Purser, and she was his passenger.

The Chief Officer on-board was a very funny and likeable character who was the spitting image of Danny De Vito. He thought that China Lil was a bit of a loon.

He was on the bridge one afternoon talking to the second officer. He happened to be talking about China Lil, not realising that she had come through the open doorway into the chart room. It was deathly quiet on the bridge, and the Chief Officer was telling the Second Officer with regard to Lil saying '"What she needs is a good sh****ng!" "Oh no I don't!" shouted China Lil from the chart room, making Duncan the Chief Officer, jump out of his skin.

Ray with other passengers and crew had gone ashore one evening in Fiji. Ray, a little worse for drink decided to take a paddle in the sea, and accidently stood on the spines of sea urchins which had imbedded themselves deeply into the soles of his feet. Some of the crew helped to carry Ray back to the ship, and at around 11pm at night whilst Donald was slumbering, there was a loud knocking on his door. Donald stumbled out to see that Ray was being carried into his day room. Donald saw the injuries, went to the medical locker for tweezers and antiseptic, returned to his dayroom, and Ray stood facing the wall with one foot raised backwards, whilst Donald dislodged the spines, it was like a farrier tending to the hoof of a horse!

On another occasion, Ray was to go ashore for an afternoon trip. It was lunchtime, and Ray had not turned up at the saloon for his lunch. Donald asked the Deck Cadet if he could search for Ray to make sure that he was okay. The cadet went to Ray's cabin, spoke to Ray and reported back. Ray had apparently broken part of his dentures. Donald went to investigate and found that Ray was in an agitated state, saying that he could not go ashore, as he had broken a set of three front lower teeth from his dental plate. He had broken them off when biting into a stick of celery. Donald had to agree that the gap in his teeth did nothing to improve his film star looks. So Donald pondered on what he could do to achieve as a solution. He hit upon the idea that super glue would save the day. Donald located the glue and re-attached the three teeth back onto the dental plate. Ray put the plate into his mouth and looking in the mirror, was very pleased with the outcome. Ray went ashore and enjoyed his afternoon sightseeing.

Two or three days passed, and it was an evening when Donald was entertaining Ray in his cabin. They were having a great evening, and between them had consumed large amounts of whisky. The picture was of two inebriated men joking and laughing together. Then Ray swears, as suddenly his three newly attached teeth fell into his glass of whisky. Donald sought to remedy the problem quickly, and brought out the tube of super glue from the drawer of his desk. He took the teeth and dental plate from Ray, and swaying, and without accurate precision, he glued the teeth back onto the plate. Ray slipped the dental plate back into his mouth and beamed like an idiot. Immediately, Donald noticed that something was wrong, as the teeth had been put in the wrong way around, and they jutted outward, so that he looked like a chipmunk. Donald asked Ray for the dental plate back, and as the glue had set the teeth, he had to smack the plate sharply against his desk, which then dislodged the teeth, sending them flying across the cabin and onto the carpet. Picking the teeth up Donald tried to super glue them, and they stuck to his fingers rather than the plate. Donald frantically flicked them off and they landed on the carpet pile again. He then super glued them into place, and asked Ray to pop them back into his mouth. Donald squinted his eyes looked at the teeth. He noticed small tufts of orange carpet pile sticking out from under the teeth. He decided not to tell Ray straight away.

Bank Line employed a permanent Superintendent to be in charge of logistics for the smooth operation of cargo being discharged and loaded at the various South Pacific ports. He was stationed in Cairns, Australia, and would stay on-board the ships when they called into the South Pacific ports. Captain Barlow was the Superintendent, he had been employed by the Bank Line for years, and knew his business well. He was a loud and confident man, and knew the power of his position, so that there was a certain swagger about him, and Master and crew would be sure to be on their best behaviour when he was on-board. Ray had his cabin on the Captain's deck at the top of the alleyway. If anyone was seated in the Captain's cabin, they had a birds eye view on anyone that passed up or down the alleyway, to and from Ray's cabin.

Donald had no idea about fashion and what the trend of the day was. So he would leave the purchase of his clothes to his wife Penny. She had packed Donald's suitcase before he left the house. Donald thought he would smarten himself up when Ray had invited him up to his cabin for a drink, so he chose a shade of pink trousers from the wardrobe in his cabin. He had never worn them before, and if it was his choice, he would have considered the trousers a little 'loud'. They certainly were not like the conservative dress code that he was used to. Anyway, Penny said that they were the fashion, so he said "What the hell", and put them on. They seemed to be baggy, but must be the fashion, he thought.

He left his cabin and made his way up to Ray's cabin, passing the Captains open doorway. The Superintendent Captain Barlow seeing this apparition, shouted after Donald saying "What the f**k! Hey what are you wearing? "What are those trousers made from? Parachute silk?" Donald turned around, but for once in his life he did not have an answer. Needless to say the trousers never saw the light of day again. They obviously weren't that fashionable then!

Donald enjoyed working with a Russian crew and had a great respect for them. If the Russian people liked and respected you, then they were loyal, true and good friends. Before this time, most people considered Russians, all to be communist, and not to be trusted. The Cold War and the Iron Curtain had caused a mutual distrust between the democratic countries and communist states. For us in the West the warning, was always 'Reds under the Beds'. A people that should be feared.

So it was with surprise that he saw that the Russian people were just like everybody else in the world. People with the same worries, the same frailties and imperfections, as the people in the West. After all, it is not the people who should be branded either a fascist or a communist, it is the politicians that are the ones that should stand alone for the country, they themselves established.

It was novel for Donald to work with women at sea. His Chief Cook, called Vladimir and went by the pet name 'Vovar' was a middle aged balding man with a quiet disposition. He could understand English reasonably well, but communication was difficult. When Donald would try to explain how to prepare and cook a certain dish. Vovar would then ask "Bottom up?" It became apparent after discussing many dishes that "Bottom up," whatever it meant, seemed to work as the end product was a tasty meal. So Donald just agreed that everything should be cooked in a bottom up style.

The rest of the catering team were a different kettle of fish. There was the second cook, who was a tall six foot and two inch blond amazon of a woman. She was intensive and her name was Irina. Donald felt immediately intimidated when Irina came close. She used to sway her hips as she wandered past Donald in the galley, and then would bend in front of him in her tight checked trousers, whilst she pummelled bread dough in the mixer.

The three stewardesses were Idalya, and then there was Lily and Anastasia. All four girls seemed to get along well together. Though Donald did feel sorry for the Chief Cook Vovar, as he didn't stand a chance with the four girls. Idalya was Donald's favourite as she was stewardess to some officers, responsible for cleaning their cabins, including Donald's. She was loyal, and would inform him of all that was going on. So Donald was well tuned to what was happening in all the departments on the ship.

The girls though did tend to upset the equilibrium. They knew all the administrative personnel that operated out of their crewing agency in Vladivostok, and took great delight in telling the senior Russian officers, together with the junior officers and ratings that they would be informed upon by them, should they step out of line. Donald found this extraordinary in that stewardesses should have the power over the ship's crew.

He asked the girls to meet him in the galley, and told them that it was unacceptable that they should bully the officers and crew in such a manner, and that they must desist from this behaviour immediately. They smiled sweetly back. Lily, then spoke out and said "But Don, we are women! How can we stop?"

There was no answer to that question.

The second cook, Irina, was intent in achieving a better working environment for herself on-board, and her plan was to seduce Donald, so that she could have her wicked way and a cushy life-style.

Donald was working in the vegetable chiller room situated on the deck below the galley. He was trimming the vegetables and giving the chiller a tidy up, busying himself and enjoying the peaceful solitude. Then he heard the chiller door open, and the elongated form of the second cook was outlined in the doorway. She shut the door behind her and walked steadily toward Donald, her hips swaying lightly from side to side in her close hugging checked pants. Donald could feel his pulse rate starting to go up, and a cold sweat had developed on his brow. "I love you Don" she said in a low husky voice as she pushed her breasts up to his face, unbalancing him into the pile of potato sacks, stacked behind him. "I want you" she said in her strong Russian accent. "You can't have me Irina" Donald said, his voice quavering. "I'm married you know!" "I don't care, we can make sweet music, just you and me, pleeease". She said.

This was going too far, and nookie was not on his mind. With a quick side step, he pushed past Irina and dashed to the door, making his escape. The episode was never mentioned again, and Irina gave up on her seduction plan.

Ray Pierrepoint was thoroughly enjoying the cruise. He was in attendance at a lot of the informal parties held in the various cabins. He had a special party piece, which he would perform when he had one over the odds. With party music playing loudly, he would ask for a couple of elastic bands, and swaying to the music, he would then proceed to pulling down his shorts, and his underwear, down to his ankles. He would then fumble with the elastic bands, and proceed to truss his penis and testicles, so that his ball we uppermost on his c**k. He said that it now had been transformed into 'Ronald the snail!' But the jumbled mass of lumps, bumps, hair, loose skin, looked more akin to a young squeaker pigeon. Onlookers were bemused at Ray's interpretation of a snail, and were not sure what to make of the unusual spectacle at all!

During the vessel's call at Lae, Papua New Guinea, there was shore leave allowed. Lae was a little like the Wild-West, in that the crime rate was high, and it could be lawless from time to time.

Ray and Donald were ashore, walking along a dusty street in Lae, on a humid and sunny day. There was then the sound of gunfire that appeared quite close. Upon walking further into the town, they noticed ahead of them, that a throng of people were massing outside a building which turned out to be a bank.

Both men joined the throng, as they were interested in what had just taken place. They had come upon a failed bank robbery, and the Police shoot-out with the bank robbers claimed the lives of the bank robbers, leaving five of them dead. Ray and Donald were lucky that they had arrived late instead, they may have been caught up in the crossfire!

The trip on the FOYLEBANK came to an end, and all of the passengers including China Lil said that they had all enjoyed the experience.

Ray kept in touch when it was time to leave the vessel. Captain John Millar, together with Chief Engineer Andy Seawater, their wives visited Donald at his home for a reunion party. Ray turned up with his wife and parked their mobile home in Donald's driveway.

On another occasion Ray and his wife turned up in their Rolls Royce, and Donald, Penny and Flick were treated to a grand day out and about in the Rolls.

Ray remained friends with the Drinkwater family for the rest of his life. Before the end of his life at the age of sixty-six, Ray rang Donald who was at home, and informed him that he had cancer, and that the condition was terminal. Donald was shocked, and hesitatingly asked Ray how long did he have? Ray in his usual upbeat and jokey manner responded "What time is it now?" Ray then told Donald "I know that you take the same shoe size as me, and I know it will mean dead man's shoes, but I want to leave you four pairs of my finest Italian leather shoes when I go." This was very humbling for Donald. When Ray did pass on a few weeks later, his wife Bernice posted the pairs of shoes to Donald. Thirty years later, Donald still has one pair of the shoes, and the pair are used for special occasions.

When Ray died. Donald wrote a poem in commemoration. The poem was put into the hearse with Ray's coffin and displayed from the funeral home to the church service.

The poem reads as follows:

A DIAMOND GEEZER
Real diamonds are few and seldom seen
And uncut stones are considered the cream
There are gems and gold, glitz galore
A diamond's so special when washed ashore

Rays is a diamond and he is a rock
A real true friend that you cannot knock
His presence and humour, his wit and his grit
Makes this man special and true, true Brit

Some people might say that Ray is a Saint
Though this in his face, you cannot paint!
He'll have you rolling in the aisle
This guy, so real with a special style!

He's never won a prize at any race meeting
Though his baby pigeon does take some beating
Ronald the snail was really never slow
It was the elastic bands that made him go!

When chomping on a celery stick
Ray broke his dentures in just a tick
Oh calamity and what can we do?
Yes, we'll fix them up with Super Glue!

Ray's a lucky man, and that's for sure
For him, there will always be an open door
His friends, so many, know and trust
That a friendship like his, will never rust!

CHAPTER SEVENTEEN
STORMY SEAS

Following more tours of duty on other vessels. Donald returned for a second voyage on the Foylebank. The crew were by and large the same people that he had sailed with over the past eighteen months. The Chief Cook was Vovar, who was a brilliant cook, there was a new Second Cook called Olga, and Donald always called her 'Olga from the Volga'. Idaylia, his favourite stewardess was still sailing with him, though by now she was in a relationship with the Russian Chief Officer, called Vladimir. There was a new Captain, a forty-something year old who quite fancied himself as a gigolo. He was a very amenable chap, and Donald got on very well with him.

The Captain had gained a reputation for being quite the womaniser, so the stewardesses had to be aware, that if he took a shine to any one of them, she may become a frequent guest in his accommodation.

The passengers joined the vessel in the port of Hull. Donald watched them as they all trooped up the accommodation ladder. Looking at this motley crowd, he thought 'this could be an interesting voyage'

First there was a British couple called Ken & Brenda. Ken was a retired teacher who was white haired and sported a trendy beard. Then there was Katherine, a short dumpy bespectacled lady, who carried a teddy bear under her arm.

Next was Dick & Jean, from the jolly old US of A. Nice couple. Then the McTaggerts, Malcolm and Yvonne. Malcolm was a top barrister from Scotland, whilst Yvonne, who wore her blond hair, bobbed on her head, looked remarkably like Bet Lynch from Coronation Street. Then there was Charles, an Octogenarian from London, a sprightly old gent. There was also Margo, who was an American lady. Last but not least was Henry & Brenda. Henry was born in Sussex but had spent many years living in Manchester. He had the poshest of all poshest voices imaginable. Whenever he spoke, it was as if he had a mouthful of gobstoppers and he talked whilst his tongue argued with the gobstoppers.

The trip was going along smoothly enough and the passengers settled down with each other. However, as most of the passengers enjoyed a tipple. This did not include passenger Kate, the psychologist who carried her teddy bear around with he everywhere. Kate was a rehabilitating alcoholic. A member of AA, was now a devout teetotaller. She had an issue with all the merry tippling that the other passengers enjoyed. The constant frowns and glares in their direction did not make her many friends. From Donald's point of view. It did not matter that she may be a raving lunatic. In his eyes, she was a paying passenger and should be treated with due respect. As she was a single traveller, Donald did his best to befriend her. She was crazy about her teddy bear, who she introduced him to Donald as her son. Donald encouraged this manic behaviour, and asked a stewardess to take a photograph of Mum Kate, Dad Donald and son Teddy, all three sitting like a happy family in Donald's cabin. Kate was thrilled that Teddy now had a new Daddy. For every boat and fire drill, the passengers had to assemble in the passengers lounge with Donald as their guardian. Donald devised a plan that would either cause humour or consternation with the other passengers. In readiness for the next fire drill, he fashioned a miniature orange life jacket that would fit Kate's teddy bear. Kate was thrilled, and she donned the jacket on Teddy, and carried him to the fire drill station. The look on the faces of the other passengers when they saw that Teddy now was also wearing a life jacket was priceless. They really thought that Kate had totally lost the plot.

When Donald had first met Kate at the welcoming party upon joining the ship. It crossed his mind that when she was standing at the bar, she did indeed look an odd shape. She seemed to be narrow at the chest area, steeply broadening into the middle. He never thought much more of it, until a month later when Kate was sunning herself on a lounger on deck. Donald sat next to her an engaged her in small talk. The conversation swung around to discussing Kate's mother, who Kate informed him that her mother had died from breast cancer. She then told Donald that in order that she would avoid contracting breast cancer, that a few years ago, she had a full mastectomy. She decided to opt for saline enhanced breasts, but the saline leaked. So she opted for implants, and unfortunately, they became mobile and had travelled to her shoulders, so she looked like she was wearing shoulder pads. By this time, she had had enough, and she informed her consultant that she did not want any other type of artificial enhancement, and that the implants were to be removed immediately, and he was just to sew the flaps down, and have done with it! So that answered Donald's initial query on why she appeared to be a funny shape.

When the ship called at Auckland, the Captain and Donald were enjoying a few whiskies in Donald's cabin one evening. The port agent came to the vessel to report a severe storm was brewing and heading for New Zealand. There was a cargo of JCB's in the hold, and numerous container were stacked on the main deck. The agent advised that it may not be prudent to set sail from the safety of the port, and that a delay of twenty-four hours would be safer. The Captain was under time constraints, and wanted to maintain the schedule, so decided that the ship would depart as soon as cargo had been completed. The ship sailed out of Auckland at around 11pm that night. Though around 4am the next morning whilst the vessel was making way across the New Zealand straits, which divides the North and South Island. The storm attacked with a vengeance, and it was truly frightening, as the ship was taking the full brunt of the weather on the broadside, which was sending the vessel into a synchronised roll. As the vessel was initially built for trading in ice, the structure of the hull and bow was meant for breaking ice, and was not best placed for this type of bad weather, so a synchronised roll meant that cargo would be prone to break from their anchorage and shift alarmingly. And this is just what it did. The Fleet of JCB's in the cargo hold broke their moorings and started to crash against the inside of the hull. Containers broke free from the top deck and toppled into the sea. By now the passengers were up and about. Well they had to be, as some were tossed out of their bunks. Donald went to see if they were all OK. He staggered to their quarters to find that Yvonne, the Bet Lynch lookalike had fallen and developed tennis elbow. The other passengers were frightened and some of the ladies were screaming. The only passenger who was calm and collected, was the nutty Kate, who was sitting in the passenger lounge in one of the chairs that had not been upturned, she was cradling Teddy and was singing and laughing happily.

Reports came that the Chief Cook investigating damage in the galley had been injured, when a heavy Hobart mixing machine had broken free and had careered across the galley, hitting him full on, breaking his leg. Donald made him as comfortable as possible, as another report came in to say that one of the Russian sailors had injured his hand, so Donald opened the medical locker and gave him first aid and a wound dressing. The situation was catastrophic. Donald decided to go the bridge and report to the Master on the injured passengers and crew. He staggered up the stairways, and managed to get to the bridge. Upon opening the door and walking into the bridge, he saw Vladimir the Russian Chief Officer and the Russian Second Officer. Donald asked where the Captain was. The Chief Officer just shrugged his shoulders and said he did not know, and that he was probably in his cabin. Donald asked the Chief Officer if the ship was safe, and if there was a way to lessen the impact. Vladimir explained that the ship was in a synchronised roll, because the weather was coming amid ships. The best way to come out of the roll, would be to change course and take the seas head on. Though the Master had to give this order.

Donald left the bridge and made his way to the Captain's cabin. He was at the Captain's open door, and was shocked to see that most of the furniture had been overturned, the TV had crashed to the deck, and the Captain was kneeling in the doorway, and picking up loose playing cards from the carpet. Donald went down to eye level with the Captain while he was still in the kneeling position, and tried to explain the injuries suffered by the passengers and crew.

He had to stop midway as he could see by the Captain's vacant and staring blue eyes that nothing he was saying was sinking in at all.
Donald got up and left the Captain, still intent on picking up the remaining playing cards off the carpet.

He made his way below to inspect the fridge spaces, and then returned to the passengers to offer any assistance. Eventually the storm abated, but the damage had been done. The ship reached the port of Noumea, which is in French Polynesia, part of the chain of ports that Bank Line visit. The damage to the vessel and cargo surpassed a million dollars. The Chief Cook had indeed broken his leg. The Cook was sent ashore for x-rays and the leg was put into plaster of paris. The Master decided that the Chief Cook would not be repatriated, and that it would be best, that he be laid up in his bed until the ship arrived in Singapore, when the cast would be removed, and he could return to the galley and take up his post. The ship now did not have a Chief Cook, and so it was down to Donald to cover the role of Chief Cook as well as his own job as Purser. He knuckled down to the task, whilst also ensuring that Vovar the Cook was served his meals in bed by one of the stewardesses.
As Donald had years of experience in the galley and other catering experience, he did not find the additional tasks impossible. All went well, and six weeks later, the ship arrived at Singapore. Donald was expecting that the Master had informed the port agents that the Chief Cook was scheduled to go ashore and see the doctor in order to verify that his broken leg had now fully mended, and the plaster cast was safe to remove. Donald was disturbed that there did not seem to be any transport arranged to take the Chief Cook to the hospital. So he called upon the Master to ask that the appointment had indeed been made. The Captain looked surprised that the Cook would need further medical attention. Donald asked that the Captain to accompany him to see the Chief Cook. They went together to the Chief Cook's cabin, and the Captain looking at the plastered leg, said "Isn't there a peephole slot in the plaster to sight the injury and see if it is fully recovered?" Donald was staggered. Whilst the Captain watched, Donald tapped the plaster all the way from the top to the bottom, saying "No slot! No opening, this plaster is solid all the way up and down!" The Master backed down, and agreed that the Cook should indeed seek professional medical

attention and advice. A car was arranged and the Chief Cook was dispatched to attend the hospital and an appointment with a doctor.

Later that day, the report came back from the hospital, the bone near to the ankle had not healed at all, in fact the plaster of paris had been set wrongly, and the foot had been set in a position that you would not know if the Cook was walking forwards or indeed backwards. The Chief Cook was admitted into hospital, where the bone was re-broken and set properly. He would then be repatriated home from Singapore to Vladivostok to convalesce.

Donald was now back in the galley running two jobs and for the trip through the Indian Ocean, through the Suez Canal and to the next port , which was Hamburg, where a relief Chief Cook walked on-board. The company was pleased that their Purser had covered two roles for such a long period, and he was rewarded with a cash bonus.

Donald enjoyed his following leave, as the trip had been a long and arduous experience.

CHAPTER EIGHTEEN
WALTER AND THE LAST TRIP

It was around this time that Donald's father Walter had a stroke. He had been living on his own since Margo had died, and one evening he collapsed in his home. There was no one in the house, and Walter had collapsed to the floor in his bedroom, and was unable to move or raise the alarm and ask for help.

However, Ronald who had been staying with his father for a short visit, returned from a night in town and found his father collapsed in the bedroom. He telephoned for an ambulance, and Walter was taken to Glan Clwyd Hospital for tests. The outcome of the tests revealed that Walter had suffered a severe stroke, which affected the whole left side of his body, leaving him paralysed on one side, and the stroke had starved him of oxygen to the brain, so that his speech had become heavily slurred.

Walter was in the hospital for a long period, and then transferred to a cottage hospital for further treatment, and a course of physiotherapy to help his condition.

When he eventually returned home, he was offered home help, and a nurse would help him to get out of bed in the morning, and make his breakfast, then returning to give him lunch, again at teatime, and the last call would be around 8pm, to help put him to bed. It was an awful period for him, as he had always been fit and active, and the immobility frustrated him, he became morose and felt sorry for himself for long periods of time.

The damage to his brain affected his mood so that he disliked Donald on a personal level more than before the stroke. On the other hand, he warmed more to his daughter Elsie and her husband Frank.

Donald and Penny made Walter welcome for short holidays at their home in Staffordshire and Donald would drive up to Bangor and collect Walter in his car for his holiday with them.

Walter was given his own room when he visited, and Donald was responsible in helping Walter with toileting, washing, clothing and helping him out of bed in the morning and putting him to bed at night. He would place a plastic carafe on a table next to Walter's bed so that Walter could urinate when he felt the urge during the night. Donald was always amazed when he went into Walter's room in the morning to find half a bucket of urine.

One cold and frosty morning Donald decided to give Walter a bath. He filled the bath with steaming hot water adding bath salts. He put on the electric wall heater, and closed the bathroom window so that Walter would not feel the cold draft from the outside wintry weather.

He then gently hoisted Walter into the bath where he hoped that the hot water would ease the aching shoulder that Walter experienced since his stroke. Donald left the bathroom, closing the door behind him, and went downstairs into the kitchen, to have a cup of tea with Penny. After around twenty to thirty minutes, Archie appeared at the top of the stairs, as he had been in his bedroom. He shouted down the stairs "Dad! Grandad's calling!" Donald looked at Penny with a sigh. She looked back at him and said "Don't look at me. You go, Old Spot is YOUR father!" Donald sighed again, and plodded up the stairs, he opened the bathroom door. He couldn't see anything, the room had steamed up as the window was shut, the electric fire was on, and the bath steamed. Donald opened the widow letting the steam out, he looked down to the bath, and saw that Walter had slumped down in the bath his face was the colour of a freshly cooked lobster, his eyes where flickering ,just before his nose was about to go under the water level. Donald grabbed the slippery Walter, under the arms and dragged him to an upright sitting position. The thought passed his mind, thinking that if he had turned up a minute or two later, poor Walter would have by then sunk lower into the bath and drowned!

Donald joined the ARUNBANK in Hull for another four month voyage around the world. This would be his last voyage, as the writing was on the wall, and the position of Bank Line, together with the role of Purser may be coming to a conclusion. Donald felt that he had better research future employment options before he was too old, and the employment market options would be more severely reduced.
He performed well on the ARUNBANK making sure that the passengers were happy. Baking birthday cakes, cutting their hair. Producing art work for their birthday cards and on-board course activity certificates, taking them on their tours, and also enjoying their company.

The Captain was Peter Staplegun, a six foot six giant of a man. He liked passengers, and was as keen as Donald in arranging new activities so to stave off boredom during the long sea passages. An old Bank Line tradition was to play horse racing on the outside deck. The six horses would be around twelve inches high and made from wood, and their wood be two large wooden dice. The horses would run along a twenty foot length of canvas and with six racing lanes.
The problem was that there were no horses, and no dice on the ship. So as a special project, Donald set about by changing the situation. He managed to procure wood from the chippy's shop, borrowing an electric jig saw. He then drew the outlines of horses onto the wood and with the smell of burning wood emitting from his cabin, Donald built the horses, and glued wooden stands to each horse. All six were numbered, and painted different colours for easy identification. He cut two blocks of wood, drilling shallow holes for the numbers, and finished the dices with black and white paint.

Donald stood back and admired his handy work. He was pleased, as they looked really professional. Captain Staplegun arranged the canvas race track, he also designed play money from a computer programme, and they called the money Arun Dollar Bills. A day at sea was open for all Officers, ratings and passengers to spend the day gambling on the horses. A buffet had been organised for lunch, and a barbeque to be held in the evening. There was lots of alcohol available, as the company allowed a budget in order to entertain the passengers. The day was a huge success and everyone participating in the horse racing.

There were other times when the ship was alongside in the French Polynesian ports. For any party to really take off, it was important that the gender balance was correct. The four ladies of the catering department were insufficient to make up the numbers, but through the agents, Donald managed to ensure that local girls from the town would bring a lot of colour and variety to any party. And indeed they did. The parties with bunting and barbeque used to go down a storm, and even the passengers appreciated the local girls joining in the fun.

Donald had applied to a crew management service company that operated from St Peter Port, the capital of Guernsey in the Channel Islands. There were many companies now operating off shore, and it was an ideal opportunity to return ashore and also keep working in the maritime industry.

Tribbey Line offered Donald a position as a Marine Personnel Officer. This job involved understanding maritime legislation and flag state procedures. Arranging the travel of seafarers to and from vessels. Ensuring that they held the correct certification.

It was again a career change, and Donald was still up for change. So a new challenge awaited him. He had to arrange to sell their home in Staffordshire, and uproot Felicity from her middle school in Brewood, also uprooting Archie from Adams Grammar School to study for his 'A' levels.

Penny was pragmatic about the move. She realised the necessity that changes in careers are sometimes unavoidable, and as everything had worked out with Donald's previous decisions, then she felt confident that a move to Guernsey, would eventually work out. She would of course miss all the friends she had made in the seven years since she had lived in Bishops Wood. The relocation package offered by the company was generous, as they had agreed to pay solicitors fees on the sale of their house and the purchase of a house in Guernsey. They would also pay for the furniture removal costs and the stamp duty on a new house purchase. In order that Donald had breathing space to sell their own home. The company were prepared to fund rented accommodation for a period of six months.

It was agreed that Donald would take his son Archie with him to Guernsey and source a high school in St Peter Port so that he could begin studying for his 'A' levels.

Penny and Flick would remain in Bishops Wood until the sale of the family home, and then they would join Donald in Guernsey.

So a new beginning and challenges await.

CHAPTER NINETEEN
LIFE ASHORE (AGAIN)

If Donald was expecting that the 'bosses' in charge of crewing vessels' where going to be more much more professional than the majority of Officers and ratings that he had sailed with over many years, then he was in for a big disappointment. He had always been impressed with the intelligence, the maritime knowledge that seafarers exhibited by carrying out their individual duties to an incredibly high standard. When Donald joined Tribbey Crewing Services (Guernsey) Ltd, he was initially impressed with the office structure, the computers and the work stations. The male staff dressed in collar and ties, the ladies wearing sensible office attire. On the surface, they did indeed really look the part.

Donald was keen to get his teeth into the complete change (again) in career. How to become a proficient and professional officer worker. Even in his early fifties, he was still as ambitious as he had been as a young man. Though, Donald had realised that throughout the varying stages of his life, society likes and favours both youth and beauty. He remembered those halcyon days when he was able to walk into a room and be totally aware that 'he could turn heads'. Unfortunately, as looks wane, and unless you are well up the ladder of the organisation, you are more perceived as a 'has been' and no matter what experience that you may have gleaned throughout your working life, there were many, struggling up the greasy pole, who were much younger, and knew best. The youth were forever attempting to reinvent the wheel. Donald would quietly look at his younger colleagues with their fancy titles, and smile, because he had been there himself. He hoped that they would make suitable haste whilst their sun shone, as they would also age, and their star would fade and wan.

Donald had always worked predominantly with men rather than women, though he had experience working with female Inspectors in the RSPCA and also the Russian girls employed by the Bank Line. Though for life in an office environment, the staffing was predominantly female. Donald thought that this would make a nice change.

Tribbey had paid for a six month rental of a holiday home property. It was a three bed bungalow. Suited for the summer months, rather than winter usage, as there was no central heating, and only small electric wall heaters throughout the building. The windows were single glazed, and the wall un-insulated, so that the bungalow was forever cold and damp during the winter months. Donald and Archie settled themselves into the bungalow. Archie was now attending a school in the capital, studying for his 'A' Levels. He made friends easily, but he did miss the private Grammar School that his Dad had made him leave. Archie was developing well into an intelligent and popular young man, though he was becoming a very discerning individual, and had developed an air of slight aloofness, and the liking for the better things in life. Donald feared that he had turned the boy into a 'Little Lord Fauntleroy!'

Donald learned about the maritime regulations that would enable him to be a successful marine manning officer. He did struggle with the office 'jargon', and as he was becoming older, he realised that he was not as quick and adept at picking up new skills as well as he had been when he was a younger man. He was therefore disappointed, when he was pressured by his colleagues. Donald throughout his working life had always believed that people learn at their own pace, and quiet encourage, coupled with a little patience, and would reap the ultimate rewards. However, this did not appear to be the mental outlook from an office environment point of view. Donald was bemused with peoples' interaction in the office, as there appeared to be an ethos of scrambling up the greasy promotion pole, and treading on others, to achieve this ambition. Was this really an acceptable practice? There was a lack of camaraderie that Donald had become used to when working at sea. He became more and more incredulous how the office team could continue and achieve a sustained success, and therefore, a guarantee that the company would survive as a crewing entity.

Donald became a competent marine officer. He was very popular with the seafarers who he was responsible in ensuring that they joined and left ships safely and with the minimum of fuss. The seafarers and Donald did speak the same language, as Donald was aware of their needs and requirements, as he himself had been a seafarer for over twenty years. However, this was a double-edged sword. He may have been popular with seafarers, but the popularity incurred envy in the workplace. Most of Donald's colleagues had never been to sea, and therefore to them, it was just another job. From Donald's point of view, the best part of the job, was the positive interaction with a seafarer either by email, or in conversation over the telephone. Donald, as did his colleagues, consider that the daily drudge of administrative work was really very boring and unfulfilling.

It was not long before Donald was rounded upon by his colleagues. Where the company policy dictated a 'no blame culture', this seemed to be by and large ignored by the workforce. Most were pleased to blame someone else for an error, rather than own up to their own misjudgement. Donald was amazed that many were quite happily do someone down, not behind their back, but directly to their face. Such was the fervour to gain favour and shine. Most extraordinary, as if this had been the normal behaviour at sea, then there would be a few swift thumps behind the ear for the offending culprit!

Of course, violence in the office workplace would not be tolerated, though open bullying is fine as long as the individual is in charge of the stick, and supported by management. Donald soon realised that maybe the transfer from his sea-going career to an office environment may have been an error of judgement. On the other hand, his employment prospects were narrowing, and procurement of any worthwhile employment for someone in their fifties was pretty slim. So as always, with the same tenacity and determination, Donald carried on.

Donald's clients where Global Marine, a cable laying company that owned a large fleet of ships. Donald was responsible for the planning of all the engineers to the various vessels, and he was also assigned six ships to arrange crew changes for the entire crew.

This particular team comprised of three men, the Manager, Donald and another marine officer called Mark. The rest of the team were seven women. The manager had his own small office. He was a chain smoking, and nervous middle aged man, his countenance was of a red mottled nature.

He did not appear in full control, and acquiesced mainly to the decisions and influence of the female staff, who held sway in matters of any importance. Donald did not respect this type of individual, as on the whole, he did not like weak people, especially if they were supposed to be in charge.

Global Marine as clients decided that they wanted to ascertain that Tribbey Line as crewing managers where liked and respected by the seafarers. There was a survey carried out with the seafarers being able to vote for the most proactive individual member of the Tribbey Global Marine team. The Managing Director of Global Marine, visited the offices of Tribbey to give a talk regarding the fleet. At the end of the talk, he announced with a great flourish, that the person nominated to be the most proactive was DONALD! The prize was a meal for two at once of the fancy restaurants in St Peter Port. Donald was thrilled as he went up to collect his voucher. There was lukewarm applause from the team. Donald thanked the Managing Director of Global Marine and returned to his seat. He felt sure that he heard the 'faint noise of people mentally sharpening their knives on a flint stone'. He was right. The knives were out, this was definitely the beginning of the end with his employment at Tribbey.

The sale of his house in Staffordshire stalled, and there was no sale in sight after six months on the market. This also ended the six month limit, where the company had been paying the rent for the accommodation in Guernsey. As Donald would have to source the monthly rental payment himself, he took on additional employment as a shelf stacker at a supermarket, working from 8pm to midnight. Tribbey also gave him a gardening job at the offices which had large grounds, so he worked four hours every Saturday gardening for £10.00 per hour. Together with the Supermarket work, he earned an additional £500.00 a month, sufficient to pay the monthly rent.

No opportunity was lost in making Donald's life as difficult as possible. Bullying knew no bounds. Eventually a case was found where Mr Ian Gatling, the department manager could arrange a formal disciplinary for Donald. It really was not Mr Gatling's making, but he was scared of his female deputies, so Donald was really the lesser of two evils.

A disciplinary was held, and Donald considered that it was more like a kangaroo court, rather than a fair trial. When Mr Gatling, who presided the meeting, and was therefore neutral in opinion, decided to berate Donald, and prove him to be a scoundrel of momentous proportions. Donald had to quietly remind him that he was supposed to be unbiased, and his outburst should be deleted from the record. Donald brought in character witnesses in his defence. But they were poo pooed, and sent out of the room. Donald was eventually found guilty as charged. His deputy had scribbled the court proceedings onto a pad of notepaper.

The notes were eventually typed up and Donald was given a copy. Donald then asked Mr Gatling, in front of his deputies "Where are the contemporaneous written notes taken at the trial?" Mr Gatling spluttered that Sonia the deputy had thrown the notes away. Donald then said "That's not the correct procedure. How do I know that the notes taken during the trial, are the same notes that you have now presented me?" Mr Gatling was without words. Donald continued, "Next time, get it right, you obviously have no idea what you are doing!" With that, Donald walked off.

He survived a few more months. The work was hard, and sometimes he worked a twelve hour day, not for any reward, but reaping abuse, rather than any thanks. So when the company lost a client, they had to reduce their workforce. The Managing Director of Tribbey asked employees who would accept voluntary redundancy. For Donald, this was manna from heaven and god-sent. He immediately put his name forward which was accepted. Donald was pleased that he was being paid to leave a company, especially as he did not consider that they were at all professional.

For the personnel who had opted for the voluntary redundancy package, staff were allowed to attend job interviews during their hours of work. Donald, wanting again to be humorous, could not resist a little fun with colleagues from his own department and workers throughout the office. So when he was asked if he had found other employment, he would tell them "Yes, I have found a great job. It's with a modelling company called ADONIS Ltd. I have been chosen as a male model. Nothing crude or sleazy!" He told them that he would be modelling cardigans and slippers. His colleagues were delighted, though of course Donald could see that it was all feigned delight. On another occasion, he told them that he had been accepted at Guernsey airport, where he would be the guy, holding the table tennis bats and guiding the aircraft to the hangar. He told one colleague" If you see me from the aircraft, please don't wave, I don't want to wave back to you, as I might send the aircraft in the wrong direction!"

Another time, he told them that he would be applying for the post of deputy manager at the café in the airport. He took the time off to attend the 'interview', but in reality went to lunch with a friend for two hours. Upon his return to the office. The female deputies huddled around his desk asking excitedly "Did you get the job?" Donald told them that he was waiting in expectation for a telephone call from the restaurant manager with a decision. Donald had arranged a scam telephone call from his friend. The phone rang, and the deputies, excited and waiting by Donald's desk let Donald take the call in silence. After a minute, Donald put the phone down. The deputies in unison said "Did you get it?" Donald replied with excitement in his voice "Yes, I got it, and I start a week after I leave here!" The girls were so please for Donald. How easy the gullible are led, thought Donald. He left the company, after completing two and a half years' service. During that period, Donald had bought a home, and the company had paid for the solicitor's fees, stamp duty and removal expenses.

Below is a poem he wrote to Tribbey in thanks, so that they could have it framed and mounted on their wall.

Alas, Tribbey Crewing Services lost the Global Marine contract soon after, and then ceased trading a few years later, thus ending their role as a crewing service management company.

MV TRIBBEY – BYE BYE
Twas on the good ship Tribbey,
That this tale begins and ends.
I joined the ship in ninety-seven.
A motley crew in many ways,
Though some are still my friends.

For the crew joining Tribbey,
The ship is safe and fast.
Decks are polished, spic and span,
And all look's made to last.

So when the vessel heads for sea,
It's time to know the crew.
As it's good to see what we shall see,
When the sea, a storm doth brew!

The ship holds nearly seventy souls.
And times have changed since days of old.
When tars and sailors stoked the coals,
Now, mostly sailorettes on-board, all told.
Shoreside Bosuns, Boudicca and Amazons
Avast ye sailors, get betwixt the fold!

It's all so new and modern, so fresh and squeaky clean,
A bold and clear new concept, a homo-sapiens dream.
Our heroines like the spider true
Swallow their mate's whole, without a chew!

Thank God our good Captain is a brave man at heart.
Such a shame that he looks more like a Dickensian Clerk.
He smiles out his orders and is bereft of true wit,
To the Amazons, a joke, and bit of a twit.

Now the good ship Tribbey is near to the rocks,
Hands are on decks, and on with their socks.
Captain and Chiefs, nowhere to be seen,
But Bosuns and Amazons, are always so keen.
Bailing out water with Bras' and panties'
They'll save the old ship, while singing sea shanties!

It's time to sign off, and a transfer in place.
Don't want to take leave, but I must make haste.
For the good ship Tribbey is now in safe hands,
She will drift quite happily, along with the flow,
Or they can bring out the oars, pull back, and row.
Good luck to Tribbey and all of her crew.
May Spring tides and fair winds,
Bring fresh trade anew.

It was around this time that Donald's father Walter was not doing at all well with his health. It was now nearly two years since his stroke. His speech remained slurred, and he was still paralysed down the left side of his body. His eyesight was also poor. Six months after the stroke, he was determined to be as mobile as possible, and there was nothing or no-one that would deter him for buying a mobility scooter. The family thought that this incentive was a disaster waiting to happen. However, Walter went ahead and bought the scooter. For his test drive, he sat on the scooter with the help of Frank, his son in law and Donald's sister Elsie. Walter started up the engine, he put his foot onto the accelerator, one hand on the handle bar, and the scooter hurtled unexpectedly up the pavement, then off the pavement, with Frank & Elsie giving chase. Walter, who had no idea if it was Christmas or New Year, was still heading for the busy main road. He narrowly missed a woman pushing a pram, a car swerved out of Walter's path. Fred and Elsie, both panting, caught up with the scooter, and brought it to a stop. That initial test drive was Walter's first and last attempt driving the contraption. He was far too dangerous to be driving on the road or a pavement. He was a danger to himself and the public. His next venture was to buy a £7,000.00 walk in bath, and this was installed into the downstairs bathroom adjacent to his bedroom. The thought process was that the hot water would sooth the constant ache in his shoulder. Unfortunately, when he managed to open the bath door, stumble in and close the door. He would sit on the plastic moulded platform inside the bath and switch on the taps. However, filling the bath was a slow process, and poor Walter would be shivering in the cold whilst the water level rose ponderously slowly. Twenty minutes later the bath water would reach the desired level. By this time, Walter was so bored of bath time, and was then wanting to come out.

Donald was aggrieved that his father Walter was still showing aggressive belligerence toward him, as Donald by this time well understood his father's nature, and had felt for a long time that both his parents had never been mentally equipped with the right tools to raise children in a normal environment. He would have liked his father to have mellowed as he moved toward the end of his life. But Walter had no intention of mending his ways. He would goad Donald, and struggling with his speech, made it perfectly clear that his prejudice remained intact. Donald would try to assure Walter, that he was not interested in any inheritance or money reward, and that his father could spend his money on whatever he wanted, and that he should not create a soap opera performance by goading one son, and praising the other. Donald's words were lost on Walter.

Walter died in hospital on 29 April, and Donald's sister Elsie telephoned him from Bangor to say that father had passed away. Frank and Elsie were very good, as they both lived in Bangor, it was easier for them to arrange the funeral. Donald and family made it to the sad occasion, and then on to the service at the crematorium. A wake was held at a large restaurant in Bangor, and mostly, close and extended family attended the passing of Walter. His ashes were interred next to those of Margo.

Donald and his family then returned to Guernsey.

Brother Ronald had also experienced a loss in that his wife, Esmeralda passed away soon after Walter. Ronald and Esmeralda had been living in the Algarve. Ronald had been a Type 1 diabetic since his late twenties and was insulin dependent. Esmeralda, had suffered from breast cancer in her younger days. It was a few months after Walter's funeral that Esmeralda noticed a lump in her breast, and fearing the return of breast cancer, she became neurotic and morose. On one hand she wanted to know a diagnosis, but on the other hand was terrified, should the diagnosis signify the return of her breast cancer? Although Ronald beseeched her to see a doctor, she refused. Then one day when Ronald was at his place of work. For some inexplicable reason, she injected herself with her husband's insulin. Ronald had been working all day, and returned home to find his wife collapsed in their hallway. He called an ambulance. She was taken to a hospital for examination and it was determined that she had become comatose. She could open her eyes, but there was very little brain function. She remained at a care home for nine months, before she contracted pneumonia, and unfortunately passed away.

Ronald was devastated with the loss of his wife, and sought consolation with his deceased wife's best friend Anna. She was a lady of wealth, owning an animal sanctuary in the Algarve. It was not before long, and Ronald had moved in with this kindly lady.

Ronald and Anna were very happy for five years. But Ronald had a wandering eye. A 35 year old kennel cleaner called Francesca, a Brazilian lady flirted with Ronald. He could not believe that this very much younger woman would be interested in him. He could not help himself, and cheated on Anna who now in her seventies was not really interested in bedroom antics.

Ronald and Francesca came up with a plan that they would leave the animal shelter under the cover of darkness, and drive to Lisbon to look for work. So one night, Ronald packed his bags with Anna totally unaware that Ronald was leaving her. Ronald and his young lover crept to his car, loaded their suitcases, and made their escape. They travelled through the night from the Algarve to Lisbon staying at a small B & B. They then searched for appropriate work, but there was no employment that would pay a decent living salary. As Portugal was part of the European Union, a lot of Portuguese nationals who had already experienced what Ronald was now learning, had been leaving Portugal for years, and seeking employment in the United Kingdom.

So Ronald decided to return to the United Kingdom and bring Francesca with him. However, he did not know, that as she was a Brazilian national, she would not be allowed entry into the United Kingdom without the appropriate visa. He did not know it at the time, but she was also an illegal immigrant in Portugal. On their arrival in the UK, he was forced to send Francesca back to Brazil, and had to dip into his own pocket for the cost of the air fare.

Ronald eventually came to Guernsey where he stayed with Donald and Penny, at their home, while he looked out for employment on the Island.

Belinda was now at the University of Wales in Aberystwyth, studying business studies and accountancy. She would come home during the holidays, and take up work at a large chemist in the town. The same chemist where Penny was working, full time in the pharmacy department, as a dispenser. Penny enjoyed the work, and the reasonable wage that she earned from the shop. Belinda took a gap year out from university, and worked in an accountancy firm. She enjoyed life on the Island, and hoped to stay in Guernsey after leaving university. She in fact, did very well indeed, as she gained a first degree. It was not unexpected, as she was always determined to be first at everything, and if she could not be first, it was not for the want of trying. Belinda was accepted for a permanent position with the accountancy firm that had her employed her during her gap year.

Belinda was never afraid of leaving a company and moving to another. She must have inherited this trait from Donald. She worked in many accountancy firms and banks. She married a man nine years her senior, and settled down to married bliss.

Archie was not the same determined trier like his older sister. He did not have to be. He was naturally bight and intelligent. He would, like most boys, leave studying to the last minute, then swot aggressively before an exam, and then pass the exam with flying colours. Archie eventually achieved good 'A' level grades, and was then accepted into Lancaster University where he studied Politics and International Relations. He achieved a 2/1 degree. He then went on to study for an extra year at the university, to gain a Master's degree. Achieving that goal. Archie had never given much though as to what he would do for a career, but during his time at Lancaster University, he decided that he would like to join the army as an officer cadet. Following the usual interviews and medicals, he was accepted as a trainee officer, and started his training course at the Military Academy at Sandhurst. Archie met with the two Royal Princes' William and Harry, as they were also studying at Sandhurst. He really enjoyed the whole experience, and made many friends. Sandhurst had moulded Archie into a well-groomed and well balanced young man. Donald and Penny were very proud of him as they were equally proud of both Belinda and Flick. They were all very successful, although different in nature, all three of them grew up with confidence in themselves, and a desire to be the best at what they can do.

Archie, passed out of Sandhurst Military Academy, and was now a Lieutenant. He served in Afghanistan on two occasions. He was promoted to the rank of Captain. After a few years, he resigned his commission and he settled down with Janet, a lovely young girl that he had met at Lancaster University. They now have two beautiful daughters.

Flick, who was a naturally intelligent and bright girl, and did well at school. She did have a rebellious streak, and Donald thought this was an unfortunate trait that she had inherited from him. But he felt sure that she would use her stubborn nature in a positive manner, which in turn would be her a success in the world. So Donald was not surprised that Flick did not want to go to university. She instead wanted to go straight out into the world of business. She did just that, and she developed a natural ability to get people to do what she wanted, without them being aware that she was pulling the strings. Flick went into the Financial Trust Industry. Her first position was as an officer junior. Quickly being promoted to assistant Trust Administrator and then a Senior Trust Administrator. In order to spread her wings and be more independent, she moved to Jersey to work in the Trust Division at a prominent bank.

God was still smiling down sideways upon Donald, as he did not have to wait for new employment too long. When he left Tribbey, he took leave for a week, and started work at another Shipping company called Chichester Maritime, operating from Saint Peter Port. This was a larger ship management company than Tribbey. Donald had been offered a position as marine manning officer. He was to stay with Chichester Maritime for a full nine years. The company was better organised that Tribbey. Though Donald found that although he had moved from one company to another, he likened the experience to leaving one theatre and joining another. The cast were virtually the same, and the shows were very similar.
He remained good friends with the Global Marine Personnel Manager, and Global Marine were disappointed that Tribbey had let Donald leave the company, as they, as clients liked Donald's performance as a crewing officer for their seafarers. The manager had informed Donald that they had paid Tribbey crewing money to be paid out as a performance bonus, and that he was due his share of the money. Donald telephoned the Managing Director at Tribbey from his new place of work. The MD was startled that Donald was now working for another crew management company and said to Donald that he thought that he was employed at the airport. Donald quickly put him straight, and was firm in advising the MD not to pocket the bonus budget, as his client (Global Marine) had instructed him to pay Donald his share, even as he was no longer employed at Tribbey.

The MD was in a corner, as he did not want to cross swords with his client, and duly sent Donald a cheque for his share of the bonus.

Donald worked on one contract for nearly three years and then transferred to another contract with a different team. It was an error of judgement as the role was incredibly boring, and the day to day tasks became a supreme effort to perform without losing one's mind. So he looked for something else that could be more challenging.

He wrote to the local bus company and asked if there was a vacancy for drivers. He received word back that they were enrolling a batch of prospective drivers for training. Donald was invited to the headquarters where he undertook a simple IQ test, together with simple arithmetic. He passed the theory, and was invited to meet on a weekend, and they would assess his driving skills. Donald drove a bus with L plates under the supervision of a qualified bus driver. He passed the practical test. He was then offered a two week 'crash' course where at the end of the course, he would take a driving test to qualify for a passenger service vehicle certificate. Donald took a two leave period from Chichester Maritime, so that he could go on the bus driving course. Things went from OK, then not so OK, then bad, to worse. The bus training instructor did not like Donald from the word go, and instead of trying to help him gain confidence, he heckled Donald at every opportunity. This constant berating undermined Donald's confidence, and by the middle of the second week, he crashed the tail end of the bus into a wall in the centre of town. Needless to say, he never got as far as the test centre. Donald thanked the training instructor, and said that he would see him around. Suffice to say, that crash, ended his bus driving dream. In hindsight, it was definitely the right outcome. Donald was a hopeless navigator, due to a poor memory for direction. He would have made a hopeless bus driver, as his passengers would have enjoyed many mystery tours rather a scheduled journey.

He was eventually promoted to Senior Manning Officer at Chichester Maritime, and even had his own clients to manage. This was a tremendous change with more positive and different work. After six years, due to his previous catering experience, he was promoted to a Catering Superintendent and responsible for the victualling budgets for two fleets. He enjoyed the role very much, as he travelled to Venezuela for a three week tour, visiting six vessels at various ports. Working with the catering departments, training and changing working procedures, which produced improved victualling results.

After nine years with Chichester Maritime, the technical department, which Donald had been transferred to from the crewing department was being closed down, and all of the technical department were to be made redundant. Donald was pleased, that yet again, he was being paid a tax free lump sum to leave a company.

God was still smiling on Donald, as lo and behold, he was offered a job with Anglo Oil Company as a manning officer with improved wages. He finished working with Chichester Maritime on a Thursday, and started his new employment with Anglo Oil on the following Monday, again at Saint Peter Port.

Figure 18 Excerpt of cartoons for the CEO retirement book

Figure 19 Excerpt of cartoons for CEO retirement book

Figure 20 Excerpt of cartoons for CEO retirement book

CHAPTER TWENTY
HEADING TOWARD RETIREMENT

The Anglo Oil Company had been in existence for nearly one hundred years. It was truly a British owned and managed Oil Company with tremendous resources.

Donald was really pleased to have been accepted with Anglo Oil, as the wages were generous, there was a fantastic pension plan, and the opportunity to buy shares at well under the market rate, whilst the company paid each employee a monthly bonus, if they were enrolled in the share scheme. They were also paying a generous annual performance bonus.

Anglo Oil only had their crewing department in Guernsey, as their offices and headquarters were in Sunbury in the United Kingdom. In Guernsey, there was only a workforce of around sixteen personnel. Donald hoped that with such a small team, that office politics would be at a minimum, as the team's client was the actual employer, and that it should be easier and less negative than the other ship management companies. How wrong he was!

The Guernsey office was ruled like a fiefdom. There was a General Manager was called Peter Baring, then two Personnel Managers called Andy Oldham and David Derringer. An Office Manager called Brenda Shelling who was married to a senior manning officer called Nelson, who in turn worked with three more seniors, named Hannah, Helga and Patricia. There was a cadet manager called Cherry Thomas, an accounts lady named Demi Titmus. There were then four crewing officers called William, Martin, Betty and of course yours truly. Finally two assistant crewing officers called Dennis and Cathy.

The General Manager was an interesting cove, who on the surface, anyone would think that he was a reasonable chap in charge. It was likely that at the onset of his position that he was relatively decent. But he, like most people, stretch the boundaries, and found himself to be in quite an enviable position, as although Anglo Oil was a powerful shipping company with modern procedures, they operated solely in the Home Counties. It was a little like when the Russians owned Alaska in the nineteenth century, and ran that part of the Russian Empire quite differently to the way it was run in Russia. In Alaska, the Russians in their comfortable solitude, would say "God is in his heavens, and the Tsar is far away!" And so it was in Guernsey, that a similar fiefdom on a miniature scale was enacted. After all, if bad practice is at the top of a hill, then like excreta, the only way it can travel is down. The team enjoyed more personnel with a managerial status and very few actual workers.
So for manning officers and assistants, they all had their work cut out, whilst the upper echelon held lots of meetings away from the shop floor.

The biggest fly in the ointment was one of the Personnel Managers. David Derringer was a man in his thirties, and he had served in the army as a commissioned officer. That was his claim to fame, as Donald measured him against his own son Archie, who had also been a commissioned officer in the army. There was a glaring disparage. Where Archie fitted the bill in many ways, he was charismatic, good looking, respected, well balanced and people were dawn to him because he exuded confidence, knowledge and ability. Poor David Derringer, on the other hand, lacked any of these attributes. He was short, stubby and balding, bespectacled, he stuttered through a conversation, and was totally bereft of any charm or charisma. He had been brought into the team to understudy the General Manager and to be promoted when old Peter resigned.

David Derringer was Donald's team manager, and although Donald endeavoured to overlook David's shortcomings, and just avoid confrontation, and carry out his own tasks. David Derringer who was always anxious to impress the General Manager with his own managerial skills, became increasingly bullish, making Donald and his colleagues, really unhappy and depressed. There was no reprieve from this man, who was immune to his own ineptitude. Every project he undertook ended in catastrophe. Even the General Manager was sometimes in despair. Though he did not want to discourage Mr Derringer, as after all, he himself had hired him, because he was a mirror image of himself. Managers, as a rule only hire people of their own ilk.

David Derringer wreaked havoc on a daily basis, but he saw himself as manager extraordinaire.

One Christmas, when the usual practice was that a 'Secret Santa' was enacted. This is when everyone is pulls the name out of a hat, and buys a present for the chosen colleague, though the giver of the present remained a secret. Donald, whose mischievous nature remained intact, decided to re-create the Secret Santa theme with a twist. He bought two management books from Amazon. One book, was just a hilarious story about survival in an office. The other paperback was the popular self-teaching advice on 'How to Win Friends and Influence People'. Donald wrapped both paperbacks separately. Andy Oldham, the personal manager in the other team would receive the humorous paperback, whilst David Derringer, would receive the manual on 'Winning Friends.' After all, he needed as much help as he could get!

David Derringer did receive his self-help book, and a cardigan. There was an enquiry as to who bought him the book, but Donald kept tight lipped for the rest of his time with Anglo Oil.

The one hero that Donald really respected, was the CEO of Anglo Oil. This man seemed to make up for all of the inadequate people that Donald had grown accustomed to. The CEO was John Bridgway. A remarkable man. He had begun his career in his early twenties as a Deck Cadet. He was from a working class family, and was born with intelligence, a photographic memory, and a drive to succeed in anything he put his mind to. He worked through the ranks becoming one of the youngest Captains in the Fleet. He moved into the office, working his way up by sheer dedication and fortitude and eventually becoming CEO. Mr Bridgway never forgot a name, and remembered every one he met. Donald was amazed how he could give a talk about the progress of Anglo Oil, by never using notes. In Donald's mind this man was like an oasis in a very dry desert. A very inspirational human being!

It was coming near to John Bridgway's retirement, and upon his last visit to the office in Guernsey, he came over to give a talk, and also to say goodbye. Donald was sorry that this great man would no longer be at the helm. As a special token to the man, Donald painted him a picture of an old Anglo Oil vessel from a photograph taken in the same year that John Bridgway was born. At the end of the CEO's talk to the team. The office manager presented the CEO with a gift from the team, and also the wrapped painting. Mr Bridgway unwrapped the painting, and his eyes moistened. He walked across the room to Donald, and hugging him, the CEO told Donald "I will never give this painting away. If anyone offered me a million pounds, I still would never give it away!" Donald was so pleased that the CEO had liked the painting. Though, he did hear the faint sharpening of knives in the room!

The assistant to the CEO who had accompanied Mr Bridgway to Guernsey telephoned the Office Manager a few days later and asked if Donald would draw some caricatures for the up and coming retirement party to be held for the CEO. He was going to be presented with a 'This is your Life' book and they wanted pictures. Donald agreed, and a secret plan went out to glean as many stories about the CEO in order to make relevant cartoons telling his story. In the end Donald painted fifty cartoon pictures for the event. In his mind John Bridgway was well worth the effort. A truly great man.

Donald continued with Anglo Oil for six years, and at sixty-five years old, he retired.

Anglo Oil (Guernsey) Ltd have since closed their office in Guernsey. If employees could have concentrated more on the work in hand, instead of navel watching and self enhancement. The health of the company could have been maintained, and possibly Anglo Oil would still have an office in Guernsey.

He was now feeling his age, although he had cycled to and from work every day for six years, he did experience aches and pains and general fatigue. He had planned well throughout his life for an adequate income from various pensions, and still owned a property in the United Kingdom along with the property in Guernsey. He had no desire to be rich, but just enough in order not to worry that his life and that of Penny, and they would not be penny pinching in old age.

There was an initial fear that the life of retirement would mean a nail in his coffin, so a month or two following retirement, Donald had secondary windows fitted into the front elevation of his home. The local manager of the double glazing firm that was national name, in the world of windows, took an interest in Donald as a salesman. Donald was assured that there was no hard selling involved, and that the work only involved a few hours a month, with a retaining wage for minimal output. This sounded too good to be true, which in fact it actually was, as anything that is too good, is usually a scam. Donald went to the training school in the UK for a week's course with twenty other sales people to learn the art of coercion. He did not enjoy the course, as the ruthless sales tactics were not what Donald wanted to practice in retirement. After the course, he returned home, and over two months, sold some windows and doors. The last straw of this doomed enterprise was when the local manager informed him that "All buyers are liars!" Donald could not believe his ears, as he believed that the customer of any business was the essential bedrock that the company stood in order to survive. He then had many arguments with the manager who refused to sack him. In the end he just had to resign.

Donald and Penny now live happily at their home in full retirement. They have an allotment, and Donald paints pictures, and exhibits his artwork on line, local cafes, and in the corridors of the local hospital.

They also enjoy visiting their two lovely granddaughters, Mae and Grace.

CONCLUSION

The aim of the book was to tell a story of a man with no particular talent, who overcome obstacles, and avoided some of the slings and arrows that can put many people off their true course in life. Donald's message is to anyone who feels oppressed and misrepresented, that they can overcome what appear to be massive hurdles in their lives. No one should be cowed by another person, everyone is equal, no better and no worse. Confront the all too many opportunists, and bullies in this world. Donald found that most bully's lack courage. Play them at their own game. The one thing they fear most is being bullied. Take some quiet enjoyment in overcoming these pygmies. Your actions will deter them from oppressing others.

For the many millions of talented and worthy people in the world who have an abundance of ability, Donald's message is 'Believe in yourself!' Whenever you become disillusioned and are filled with despair, reflect back on the timeless words depicted in DESIDERTA and your sense of balance and awareness will be revived. 'You are a child of the Universe, like the trees and the stars, you have a right to be here!'

Live your lives to the full, enjoy the time that God has given you. Life is so fleeting, don't waste too much time on negative reflection, and concentrate on the positives, as the positives heavily outweigh the negative aspects of your life.

Think on whether Donald was the instrument of his own conflicts, or was he an ultimate achiever? Not everyone would enjoy constant conflict, but be prepared, and be ready to overcome conflict, when it threatens your values and beliefs.

Donald's message is that you should enjoy life and make the best of it, and your legacy will live beyond your own demise to benefit future generations.

'Good Luck'

DEDICATION

This book is dedicated to Donald's three children. Belinda, Archie and Felicity. All three inspired Donald so that his story could be written. The three are all individual characters, but they all bear the hallmark of confidence and success. Donald and Penny are both proud of all of their children, and grandchildren

Printed in Poland
by Amazon Fulfillment
Poland Sp. z o.o., Wrocław

57873030R00114